Based on Rosalind's extensive experience as a psychologist, teacher and therapist, this very readable book does more than make a compelling, evidence-backed case for the role of teamwork in improving children's communication; it provides a flexible programme of practical and creative activities to support teachers to make teamwork part of their everyday classroom practice.

Rob Webster, *Associate Professor, Centre for Inclusive Education, UCL Institute of Education*

An excellent book published at a very important time – a must-have for all those working in the field of SEND. This book not only explores the speech and language difficulties that children and young people may have but it also gives ideas, strategies and activities that will support inclusive teamwork

Lorraine Petersen OBE, *Educational Consultant*

Inclusive Teamwork for Pupils with Speech, Language and Communication Needs

This book provides a rationale for teaching inclusive teamwork and for understanding communication as a collective endeavour. It shows how teamwork can be taught within schools and emphasises the role that classmates have in facilitating good communication, particularly in the face of difficulty.

Grounded in evidence from hours of therapy and analysis of children's accounts of communication and children's interactions with their peers, the book explores the components of teamwork by looking carefully at the way schoolchildren really interact. It draws on research from the fields of education, psychology and speech and language therapy to propose the framework for a programme suitable for children aged 7 to 14 years, designed to include pupils with speech, language and communication needs. The programme includes activities, a set of criteria to use as an outcome measure and examples of the way that children and young people have responded in practice. In using the inclusive teamwork programme outlined in this book, teachers have the potential to support all children in developing rapport, effective communication and problem-solving skills.

Providing a framework designed to meet the needs of all learners, this book will be highly relevant reading for students of education, speech and language therapy and educational psychology, as well as speech and language therapists and practitioners in the field of education.

Rosalind Merrick is a speech and language therapist and psychologist, specialising in work with children with speech, language and communication needs in mainstream schools. She has a PhD in Children's Views and Speech and Language Therapy.

Routledge Research in Special Educational Needs

This series provides a forum for established and emerging scholars to discuss the latest debates, research and practice in the evolving field of Special Educational Needs.

Books in the series include:

Adult Interactive Style Intervention and Participatory Research Designs in Autism
Bridging the Gap between Academic Research and Practice
Lila Kossyvaki

The Global Convergence of Vocational and Special Education
Mass Schooling and Modern Educability
John G. Richardson, Jinting Wu, and Douglas M. Judge

Job Satisfaction of School-Based Speech-Language Pathologists
Insights to Inform Effective Educational Leadership
Kimberly A. Boynton

Families Creating Employment Opportunities for Individuals with Developmental Disabilities
Understanding the Contribution of Familial Entrepreneurship
Jennifer Percival

Inclusive Teamwork for Pupils with Speech, Language and Communication Needs
Rosalind Merrick

Social and Dialogic Thinking and Learning in Special Education
Radical Insights from a Post-Critical Ethnography in a Special School
Karen A. Erickson, Charna D'Ardenne, Nitasha M. Clark, David A. Koppenhaver, and George W. Noblit

For more information about this series, please visit: www.routledge.com/ Routledge-Research-in-Special-Educational-Needs/book-series/RRSEN

Inclusive Teamwork for Pupils with Speech, Language and Communication Needs

Rosalind Merrick

Routledge
Taylor & Francis Group

LONDON AND NEW YORK

First published 2022
by Routledge
2 Park Square, Milton Park, Abingdon, Oxon OX14 4RN

and by Routledge
605 Third Avenue, New York, NY 10158

Routledge is an imprint of the Taylor & Francis Group, an informa business

© 2022 Rosalind Merrick

British Library Cataloguing-in-Publication Data
A catalogue record for this book is available from the British Library

Library of Congress Cataloging-in-Publication Data
A catalog record for this book has been requested

ISBN: 978-1-032-06314-0 (hbk)
ISBN: 978-1-032-06317-1 (pbk)
ISBN: 978-1-003-20171-7 (ebk)

DOI: 10.4324/9781003201717

Typeset in Times New Roman
by Apex CoVantage, LLC

Contents

Tables

Introduction

Being part of a collaborative group is a factor in well-being, particularly for children and young people as their social identity develops. Moreover, engaging in positive peer interaction has significant educational benefits. This book is about teamwork – working collaboratively with a partner or small group to achieve common goals. It is also about inclusion – facilitating participation from all members of the team, so that children with speech, language and communication needs (SLCN) and classmates work enjoyably and effectively together. Inclusive teamwork has several dimensions: the children involved are relating to each other, talking and organising their efforts.

This book presents a simple but rarely recognised idea: you can teach teamwork to children, and if the team includes children with communication difficulties, all the participants benefit. Despite its apparent simplicity, implementing the idea requires a transformation in traditional approaches to education and to communication difficulty.

Communication difficulty is a reality for a considerable number of schoolchildren, and it can be understood in different ways. The medical approach is to diagnose communication disorder, the specific terms of which range from *speech sound disorder* and *language delay* to *developmental language disorder* and *social communication disorder*. The educational approach is to identify SLCN with a view to planning how these will best be met through special educational provision. SLCN is an umbrella term:

> Children and young people with speech, language and communication needs (SLCN) have difficulty in communicating with others. This may be because they have difficulty saying what they want to, understanding what is being said to them or they do not understand or use social rules of communication. The profile for every child with SLCN is different and their needs may change over time. They may have difficulty with one, some or all of the different aspects of speech, language or social communication at different times of their lives.
>
> *Special Educational Needs and Disability Code of Practice*
> (Department for Education & Department for Health and Social Care, 2015, p. 97)

DOI: 10.4324/9781003201717-1

In this book, I will use the terms *communication difficulty* and *SLCN* interchangeably. The focus of the book is on children's experience of communication and the way that needs are understood and responded to by peers in everyday interactions. Consistent with the UK Special Educational Needs and Disability Code of Practice (cited earlier), SLCN is not used here to include hearing impairment or learning difficulty as a primary need, although these may overlap. Needless to say, there are many formal diagnoses within these broader categories, and referral should be made to a speech and language therapist wherever communication difficulty is suspected or evident, in order to gain a full and accurate understanding of a child's communication profile.

What is important but often overlooked is that the communication difficulties of children with SLCN are shared by their conversational partners. Classmates can be baffled, irritated, amused or intrigued by peers who have difficulty expressing themselves and/or understanding. Whatever their reaction, they appreciate and benefit from support and encouragement in solving communication problems.

The book is written with reference to children and young people aged between 7 and 14 years. This period spans considerable development in language and social skills. The nature of peer interaction is also typically shifting during this time, with the role of the peer group tending to increase in importance. The ability and willingness to reflect on one's own interaction is something which tends to increase with maturity. As young children with SLCN grow up into teenagers, some problems resolve over time, others emerge, become exacerbated or manifest themselves in quite different ways. Support with peer interaction and collaborative working is relevant and important throughout this period, both for children with SLCN and for their classmates.

Researching children's views of communication

I am a psychologist, teacher and children's speech and language therapist. I have worked for over 20 years with children and young people with communication difficulties between the ages of 2 and 16 years in the United Kingdom, in nurseries and schools as well as in their own family homes. Since 2004, I have been working closely with children and young people with communication difficulties and their peers. I have carried out research regarding their views, explored how therapy and educational provision can be person-centred, and tailored therapy programmes to meet the needs of this client group. During my own research, 12 children who were receiving speech and language therapy were consulted about their experience of therapy and communication (Owen, Hayett, & Roulstone, 2004); 33 schoolchildren participated in group interviews on the topic of communication; and 11 children with communication difficulties participated in in-depth qualitative research using innovative methods (Merrick, 2014; Merrick, McLeod, & Carroll, 2019; Merrick & Roulstone, 2011).

I learned a great deal from the children and young people and wrote my doctoral thesis on children's views of communication and speech and language therapy. The studies made me think twice about the work that we were doing as speech and language therapists and the approach that we were taking to SLCN in schools. Outlined below are some of the things we have learned about what children say.

From children's point of view, it makes perfect sense to integrate the help that they need with communication into their school day. We discovered that children receiving speech and language therapy at school were not necessarily differentiating it from other aspects of their education. One boy said about his therapy (Owen et al., 2004, p. 63):

> It just helps my brain, that's what school's about. You go to school to learn stuff.

The children were focused on how *normal* it was to learn, rather than how *abnormal* it might be to have a communication impairment. Moreover, the children were not focused on themselves. They liked to consider their helpfulness to others, despite therapy traditionally positioning them as recipients of help, and they liked working in a group.

I listened closely to what the children were saying, those with communication difficulties and their peers, about communication, about what was problematic and what was helpful. I discovered that there were different strands – we could call them 'discourses' – and the children switched between them. They had an understanding of communication impairment – something *wrong* – but there were other ways of seeing communication available to them too, positive discourses about learning and choice. It became clear that if speech and language therapy confined itself to the discourse of impairment, it would miss opportunities to connect with children, to treat them in the way that they wished to be treated, and to make the differences that really mattered to them.

Despite increased recognition of the value of working from a person-centred perspective, the majority of teachers still struggle to involve children and young people in planning provision to the extent that they would like (Merrick, 2020). Communication difficulties pose a particular challenge even for experienced teachers in this respect. I have found reflective observation to be the key to this problem. It is always worth listening carefully to children, to the terminology they are using and the concepts that are bound up with this, noticing the choices they are making non-verbally too, and engaging with them on these terms. Throughout this book I will make reference to the comments of the children and young people that I have worked with in my research and in my speech and language therapy practice, both those with communication difficulties and their peers. These offer a continually fresh perspective on what communication, especially peer interaction, can really mean.

The value of inclusive teamwork

In common with all children, those with SLCN are hindered by victimisation and marginalisation but helped by participation and inclusion. Traditional approaches to therapy have focused on identifying impairment in individual children and tailoring adult support (individual therapy, group work or teaching strategies) to address specific deficits. From the perspectives of children with SLCN, however, social participation with their peers is a top priority. They are looking for changes in functional communication and patterns of interaction, and a positive social identity, changes which impairment-focused work may not address at all.

The quality of children's teamwork in class, and children's proficiency in including children with communication difficulties in their activities, is not currently measured or addressed. Yet teamwork is desirable and fun for children, and a worthy educational goal. Indeed, empathy and collaboration are vital across whole schools, for community, well-being, academic achievement and citizenship. When schoolchildren are taught to work collaboratively, there are significant changes not just in their teamwork skills but also in the quality of their language and thinking. It improves employability and is a resilience factor for mental health. Teamwork can be taught in a way which includes children with communication difficulties and benefits all children.

This book explores the dimensions of teamwork, looks carefully at the way schoolchildren really interact, and proposes meaningful and measurable outcomes for teachers to work towards. This process is supported by theories of learning and collaboration, what children can do and what can go wrong. Through this we understand what is desirable and possible when talking with children about teamwork. Drawing on current thinking in the fields of education, psychology and speech and language therapy, the framework is proposed for a programme suitable for children aged between 7 and 14 years.

Outline of the chapters

Chapter 1 describes communication as a collective endeavour and communication difficulty as a public health concern which all members of society have a role in addressing. It looks at the model of communication disability in society, and the part conversational partners play in facilitating good communication. Teachers and pupils can be empowered to meet SLCN in a social context by promoting inclusive child–child teamwork in the classroom.

Chapter 2 draws attention to the high number of children with SLCN in mainstream schools, the range of difficulties they have and the importance to children of participation with others. Drawing on qualitative research findings, it reveals how children themselves talk and think about communication difficulty, and the kind of assistance that really helps from their point of view. It highlights the strengths and limitations of traditional approaches to social skills training and summarises what we know about working with children on their own interaction with peers.

Chapter 3 describes the mechanisms by which children learn when they are collaborating with each other. They learn to get on with each other, to talk and to think in new ways. Relationships and good communication are not just the desired outcomes but also the tools by which children engage in learning and develop in their thinking. The chapter explores the part that adults can play in preparing children for effective teamwork and coaching them, and makes the case for teamwork which is inclusive of children with communication difficulties.

Chapter 4 examines children's outcomes (mental health and social and emotional adjustment) and the central role played by communication. Social connectedness is a fundamental human need, and we are motivated by a desire for positive interactions with others. It is common for children with communication difficulties to be subjected to marginalisation and victimisation. SLCN are associated with a decline in well-being and quality of life over time. Evidence for the association between language disorder and poor mental health and social and emotional outcomes is particularly strong. Nevertheless, children with communication difficulties can enjoy the benefits of social interaction and friendship, and this has the potential to mitigate the risks for them of poor psychosocial outcomes. According to the World Health Organization model, participation is crucial to our health and functioning.

Chapter 5 sets out an analysis of inclusive teamwork in terms of three dimensions: *Enjoy, talk* and *achieve*. It explores how these dimensions correspond with models of teamwork from education, speech and language therapy and psychology. It also looks at the way in which children develop awareness of their own inclusive teamwork and the motivation to work well as a team and to improve levels of collaboration.

Chapter 6 provides a framework for teaching inclusive teamwork. The structure for the programme is set out, outlining timescales, participants and the role of the teacher, and providing ideas for activities, which have aspects of effective communication as intrinsic to successful completion. Ideas for activities are organised according to their underlying rationale and objectives. A set of criteria is provided, by which to measure a baseline and outcome, and which serves as a tool for discussion with the children during a course of sessions.

References

Department for Education, & Department for Health and Social Care. (2015). *Special Educational needs and disability code of practice: 0–25 years* (Ref: DFE-00205-2013). Retrieved from www.gov.uk/government/publications/send-code-of-practice-0-to-25

Merrick, R. (2014). *Picture me: Children's views of speech, language and communication needs.* Guildford: J&R Press.

Merrick, R. (2020). Pupil participation in planning provision for special educational needs: Teacher perspectives. *Support for Learning, 35*(1), 101–118. https://doi.org/10.1111/1467-9604.12288

Merrick, R., McLeod, S., & Carroll, C. (2019). Innovative methods. In R. Lyons & L. McAllister (Eds.), *Qualitative research in communication disorders: An introduction for students and clinicians.* Guildford: J&R Press.

Merrick, R., & Roulstone, S. (2011). Children's views of communication and speech-language pathology. *International Journal of Speech-Language Pathology, 13*(4), 281–290. https://doi.org/10.3109/17549507.2011.577809

Owen, R., Hayett, L., & Roulstone, S. (2004). Children's views of speech and language therapy in school: Consulting children with communication difficulties. *Child Language Teaching and Therapy, 20*(1), 55–73. https://doi.org/10.1191/0265659004ct263oa

1 Communication as a collective endeavour

Communication is crucial to social relationships, school achievement and quality of life. For everyone, therefore, overcoming communication difficulties is a valuable life skill. Moreover, learning to communicate with the diverse members of one's community helps to promote the richness of that community.

People who share ideas – *conversational partners* – also share the role of facilitating good communication. Rix (2015), in a critique of special educational provision across 50 countries, concluded that there were children who were marginalised within each system, because inequality has longstanding cultural and historical origins. Reducing the marginalisation of children with SLCN requires a cultural shift, so that the onus is no longer solely on the children to acquire skills and fulfil expectations. Their listeners, and indeed the society at large, can adapt, accommodate and accept. It is in all of our interests to do so. I argue that adaptation involves mastering all the dimensions of inclusive teamwork, something that the classmates of children with identified SLCN, with the right support, are well-placed to do.

The shared task of teachers and speech and language therapists

A high proportion of schoolchildren are considered to have some form of communication disorder. More than 1.4 million children and young people in the United Kingdom are reported to have SLCN (ICAN, 2018). The inclusion agenda is prevalent in many countries (Armstrong, Armstrong, & Spandagou, 2010), and the UK Government is committed to inclusive education, that is, the removal of barriers to learning and participation in mainstream education (Department for Education & Department for Health and Social Care, 2015). However, children with SLCN do not consistently experience inclusion in schools. They are more likely than typically developing children to lack friendships, to experience bullying and to receive individualised help rather than engage in mixed-ability group work. For children with communication difficulties, this leads to a spiral of disadvantage, as they miss language learning opportunities and lack the resilience factors to cope with adversity later in life. None of this need be the case. There are examples of children

DOI: 10.4324/9781003201717-2

with communication difficulties who have good friendships and collaborate well with their classmates, and the school community benefits.

Since speech and language therapists tend to work with school-age clients in school settings, they usually consider the children's communication needs in that educational and social context (Dockrell, Lindsay, Roulstone, & Law, 2014). Teachers, meanwhile, are also aware of their role in fostering good spoken language skills as part of high-quality teaching. In England, the *Special Educational Needs and Disability Code of Practice* (Department for Education & Department for Health and Social Care, 2015) stipulates that a teacher should 'retain responsibility for' each child with special educational needs (SEN) in their class, and plan and assess how support 'can be linked to the classroom teaching' (6.52). Worldwide, it is the case that children's developing speech, language and communication are relevant to the role and responsibility of teachers.

While the benefits of pupils' good communication are well-understood, it can be challenging for teachers to know how to foster this (Dockrell et al., 2014). Speech and language therapists, with their pre-service training in linguistics, have a valuable role to play in sharing knowledge in a format that teachers can access; equally, speech and language therapists need to keep learning from teachers about the materials and information that are truly relevant (McCartney & Ellis, 2013). Indeed, children stand to gain when teachers and therapists combine their knowledge about child development and diversity, pool their creative resources and share their insights into pupils' interests, wishes and strengths.

The extent to which teachers and speech and language therapists work together varies; it depends on the structural arrangement of services and on the strength of relationships (with each other and with the pupils and their families). This has been described as a continuum: first *co-operation* through basic information sharing; second *collaboration* through joint planning; third systematic *co-ordination*; and fourth *integration* of services (Davis, 2011). One of the most common models of collaboration is consultancy, where therapists offer advice and guidance to teachers on appropriate goals and how to attain them, and it is the role of education staff to put these into practice. There are, however, examples of a greater degree of collaboration than this. When teachers and therapists coordinate their expertise, take a client-centred perspective and integrate their work, there are agreed aims, common goals and a sharing of knowledge. In this case, it could arguably be *either* a member of therapy *or* teaching staff who implements the plan.

The presence of therapeutic interventions in the school context is not without criticism. Ecclestone and Hayes (2009, 2019) urge us to keep the *pursuit of knowledge* as the focus of education. They warn against a 'therapeutic ethos' which can in fact undermine autonomy and resilience and promote preoccupation with the self. We are indeed losing sight of the function of education if we make happiness our goal (Frawley, 2015). In doing so, we are likely to become inappropriately prescriptive about how children should feel and react. (It's OK to be grumpy!) Therapeutic interventions also run the risk of over-emphasising the role of the individual, when some issues are clearly social and political (Brunila, 2012).

Positive psychology is relevant to education to the extent that it supports learning. I would add that learning to collaborate and to communicate well with all manner of partners is an important outcome of time at school, as well as an essential means by which to achieve academic outcomes. Monkman (2017) found that teachers embraced it as part of their educational role and responsibility to develop positive relationships and to support their students, but also that this depended on the language used. A medicalised discourse had the effect of alienating and disempowering teachers, so that they felt issues were best left to specialists. However, teachers also saw themselves as caring, wanting to help, in a position to know what makes their students 'tick' and what they enjoy, and able to support students' well-being. Teachers were most proactive in finding solutions for their students' mental health issues when they drew on the language of behaviour rather than pathology.

The approach proposed in this book assumes a degree of collaboration between the teacher and a speech and language therapist. For succinctness, the adult implementing the work is referred to as the *teacher*, but as stated above, the facilitator could equally be a speech and language therapist, teaching assistant, or speech and language therapy assistant. The teacher usually knows his/her pupils as well as the demands of the curriculum. A speech and language therapist will have the expertise necessary to assess SLCN and analyse functional aspects of communication. Inclusive teamwork may therefore provide a way of meeting universal, targeted and even specialist SLCN. However, it does not preclude the need for individual assessment and consideration of other forms of intervention. If a programme is implemented by an assistant, it is well-recognised that they will require appropriate *deployment*, adequate training in how to *practise* (in particular how to interact with pupils), and consistent support with time to *prepare* and share feedback (Webster, Russell, & Blatchford, 2016).

The reality in many schools is that speech and language therapy resources are highly limited. In the United Kingdom, the recommendation of a tiered approach for services means that only children with the most complex and pervasive problems are candidates for direct speech and language therapy (Ebbels, McCartney, Slonims, Dockrell, & Norbury, 2019; Gascoigne, 2006). High-quality teaching and education-led programmes are the medium of help for the vast majority of school-aged children with communication difficulties. Despite long-standing recognition of its importance (McCartney, 1999), inter-professional collaboration is still dogged by lack of a shared understanding and lack of governance (ICAN, 2018). A way through this is for professionals to align themselves better with the ideals of children with communication difficulties. We know that these children care deeply about their social participation and a supportive environment (Gallagher, Murphy, Conway, & Perry, 2019).

This book argues that with the benefits of a well-developed programme, education staff can naturally and effectively make a difference to teamwork in the classroom. Teachers can coach children on how to improve communication and include children with SLCN, providing experiences and opportunities that make a vital difference to all children, even those with a high level of need.

A public health approach to communication

Individualised therapy has an important role to play and can effect meaningful change in children's lives. Yet we need to expand our thinking. Whenever we view communication as something for which certain individuals receive rehabilitation, we miss a really important point. Communication is a collective endeavour and a public health concern, which all members of society have a role in addressing (Law, Reilly, & Snow, 2013).

There are several strands to this argument. First, it is grounded in the social model of disability. Impairment is experienced as disability when activity and participation are restricted. Access to buildings can be facilitated for wheelchair users, and so too can participation be facilitated for those with communication difficulties, by the provision of a conducive environment. For example, it is easier for a child to understand a verbal statement when the meaning is also demonstrated. It is also easier for a child to find the right words when their partner is listening but not pressuring them. The disabling effect of communication impairment is intensified by the extent to which success in our society is dependent on specific verbal skills. There have been great artists, scientists and entertainers who were not known for their spoken skills. Whenever we as a community value the qualities and utilise the skills that people with communication difficulties have to offer, their disability is reduced.

Second, not everyone seeks help; less than one-third of the children with communication difficulty are referred for therapy. Access to services is uneven, affected by such factors as geographical location, socio-economic status, linguistic community and mental health. The irony is that communication is, at the same time, basic to many of the resilience factors that help people to cope with adversity. The reality is that many children with significant and pervasive communication difficulties, because of limited access to services, stand to benefit only from learning opportunities that are available in their everyday environment. Educational inclusion takes on a new significance in this context.

Third, many problems and their repercussions are preventable. Communication difficulties can affect anyone, but they have a higher incidence in areas of social deprivation (Alsford et al., 2017; Law, McBean, & Rush, 2011). Limitations on resources have led to intervention for SLCN being focused on children's early years, when signs and symptoms may first become apparent. However, the potential for prevention work extends beyond this period. Communication disorders change in the way they manifest themselves over time; new issues arise and old difficulties persist. We can promote health and prevent impact of a condition at each stage in the child's journey by educating others to improve the environment and enable participation. Speech and language therapists are 'an untapped spring of prevention expertise' in relation to mental health and well-being (Law et al., 2013, p. 491). Expertise in creating communication-supporting environments should be deployed at a population level, with far-reaching benefits.

Communication as a shared responsibility

Communication is a collective endeavour and a shared responsibility. To take one example, intelligibility depends on the skill and familiarity of the listener as well as on the clarity of the speaker. When McCormack, McLeod, McAllister, and Harrison (2010) asked children about what it was like having speech impairment, they told the researchers about others' failure to 'listen properly'. All parties were experiencing frustration, and solutions lay with both speaker *and* listener. Those close to a person with communication difficulties are often working hard to troubleshoot so that the other person can understand and be understood, and they are emotionally invested in facilitating communication.

For adults with acquired aphasia, there are *communication partner programmes* (Turner & Whitworth, 2006). In these programmes, a relative or volunteer receives coaching along with the person with aphasia, *each* of the partners learning compensatory strategies that they can adopt to promote conversational interaction. These programmes result in more effective communication, and people with aphasia themselves report positive changes in their relationships, self-confidence and sense of identity (McMenamin, Tierney, & Mac Farlane, 2015).

Less attention has been given to the conversational partners of schoolchildren, and this is an oversight that this book seeks to address. Knowing how to communicate and collaborate effectively with a range of team members, either instinctively or consciously, is a great skill to have and, one might argue, it is essential to citizenship. All children bear the rights to act and to participate in society, and bound up with these are the rights to provision and protection (Verhellen, 2015). SEN are typically understood in terms of individual difficulty – difficulty, that is, in doing things in what has become regarded as the *normal, proper* or *appropriate* way. However, an overly individualised view fails to celebrate diversity and capitalise on the community of learning within the classroom. Florian (2014) wished to challenge 'education's normative centre' (p. 4) and the assumption that what is unusual is less than ideal. She believed that in a truly inclusive classroom, what *everyone* needs should be 'ordinarily available' (p. 7). So, for example, she suggested that the teacher present the whole class with a range of differentiated lesson options. I would extend this argument to suggest that the classroom community as a whole needs a repertoire of ways of facilitating effective communication with each of its members.

The next chapter considers some of the high-incidence communication difficulties that children have in mainstream schools, and the evidence that we have of the importance to children of social participation. It offers a review of current social skills programmes and highlights the advantages of inclusive teamwork over an impairment-focused approach.

References

Alsford, E., Ralephata, A., Bolderson, S., Curtin, M., Parish, E., Klaber, V., . . . & Pring, T. (2017). The wrong side of the tracks: Starting school in a socially disadvantaged London borough. *Child Language Teaching and Therapy*, *33*(2), 145–156. https://doi.org/10.1177/0265659016654954

Armstrong, A. C., Armstrong, D., & Spandagou, I. (2010). *Inclusive education: International policy and practice*. London: SAGE.

Brunila, K. (2012). From risk to resilience. *Education Inquiry*, *3*(3), 451–464. https://doi.org/10.3402/edui.v3i3.22046

Davis, J. M. (2011). *Integrated children's services*. London: SAGE.

Department for Education, & Department for Health and Social Care. (2015). *Special educational needs and disability code of practice: 0–25 years* (Ref: DFE-00205-2013). Retrieved from www.gov.uk/government/publications/send-code-of-practice-0-to-25

Dockrell, J., Lindsay, G., Roulstone, S., & Law, J. (2014). Supporting children with speech, language and communication needs: An overview of the results of the Better Communication Research Programme. *International Journal of Language & Communication Disorders*, *49*(5), 543–557. https://doi.org/10.1111/1460-6984.12089

Ebbels, S., McCartney, E., Slonims, V., Dockrell, J., & Norbury, C. (2019). Evidence-based pathways to intervention for children with language disorders. *International Journal of Language & Communication Disorders*, *54*(1), 3–19. https://doi.org/10.1111/1460-6984.12387

Ecclestone, K., & Hayes, D. (2009). Changing the subject: The educational implications of developing emotional well-being. *Oxford Review of Education*, *35*(3), 371–389. https://doi.org/10.1080/03054980902934662

Ecclestone, K., & Hayes, D. (2019). *The dangerous rise of therapeutic education* (2nd ed.). London: Routledge.

Florian, L. (2014). Reimagining special education: Why new approaches are needed. In L. Florian (Ed.), *The SAGE handbook of special education* (Vol. 2, pp. 9–22). London: Sage.

Frawley, A. (2015). Happiness research: A review of critiques. *Sociology Compass*, *9*(1), 62–77. https://doi.org/10.1111/soc4.12236

Gallagher, A. L., Murphy, C.-A., Conway, P. F., & Perry, A. (2019). Engaging multiple stakeholders to improve speech and language therapy services in schools: An appreciative inquiry-based study. *BMC Health Services Research*, *19*(1), 226–217. https://doi.org/10.1186/s12913-019-4051-z

Gascoigne, M. (2006). *Supporting children with speech, language and communication needs within integrated children's services*. RCSLT Position Paper. London: RCSLT.

ICAN. (2018). *Bercow: Ten years on: An independent review of provision for children and young people with speech, language and communication needs in England*. London: ICAN.

Law, J., McBean, K., & Rush, R. (2011). Communication skills in a population of primary school-aged children raised in an area of pronounced social disadvantage. *International Journal of Language & Communication Disorders*, *46*(6), 657–664.

Law, J., Reilly, S., & Snow, P. C. (2013). Child speech, language and communication need re-examined in a public health context: A new direction for the speech and language therapy profession. *International Journal of Language & Communication Disorders*, *48*(5), 486–496.

McCartney, E. (1999). Barriers to collaboration: An analysis of systemic barriers to collaboration between teachers and speech and language therapists. *International Journal of Language & Communication Disorders*, *34*(4), 431–440. https://doi.org/10.1080/136828299247379

McCartney, E., & Ellis, S. (2013). The linguistically aware teacher and the teacher-aware linguist. *Clinical Linguistics & Phonetics*, *27*(6–7), 419–427. https://doi.org/10.3109/02699206.2013.766763

McCormack, J., McLeod, S., McAllister, L., & Harrison, L. J. (2010). My speech problem, your listening problem and my frustration: The experience of living with childhood speech impairment. *Language, Speech and Hearing Services in Schools, 41*, 379–392.

McMenamin, R., Tierney, E., & Mac Farlane, A. (2015). Addressing the long-term impacts of aphasia: How far does the Conversation Partner Programme go? *Aphasiology, 29*(8), 889–913. https://doi.org/10.1080/02687038.2015.1004155

Monkman, H. (2017). The teacher's role in supporting student mental health. In A. J. Williams, T. Billington, D. Goodley, & T. Corcoran (Eds.), *Critical educational psychology* (pp. 146–156). Chichester, West Sussex: Wiley-Blackwell.

Rix, J. (Ed.). (2015). *Must inclusion be special? Rethinking educational support within a community of provision.* London: Routledge.

Turner, S., & Whitworth, A. (2006). Conversational partner training programmes in aphasia: A review of key themes and participants' roles. *Aphasiology, 20*(6), 483–510. https://doi.org/10.1080/02687030600589991

Verhellen, E. (2015). The convention on the rights of the child: Reflections from a historical, social policy and educational perspective. In W. Vandenhole, E. Desmet, D. Reynaert, & S. Lembrechts (Eds.), *Routledge international handbook of children's rights studies* (pp. 43–59). London: Taylor & Francis Group.

Webster, R., Russell, A., & Blatchford, P. (2016). *Maximising the impact of teaching assistants: Guidance for school leaders and teachers* (2nd ed.). London: Routledge.

2 Speech, language and communication needs (SLCN) through children's eyes

There are a high number of children with SLCN in our schools, with a range of difficulties. Some are educated in special schools or special support centres. However, a large number of children with diverse communication needs study full time in mainstream schools. SLCN may accompany another condition, but are often specific and without an obvious aetiology. Schoolchildren, therefore, are used to having classmates whose communication is, in some way or other, not typical. Participation with others is a top priority for them. This chapter shares findings about how children talk and think about communication difficulty and assistance. It highlights the strengths and limitations of traditional approaches to social skills training and summarises what we know about working with children on their own interaction with peers.

Children's top priorities

Schoolchildren care about communication. As a researcher and as a therapist, whenever I have engaged with children and young people and their parents, they have told me that friendships are among the greatest sources of fun and support, and that rejection is among the most painful experiences they endure. Participation in social activity is a number one priority for outgoing and shy children alike. Below are really simple, clear comments from an 11-year-old girl with high-level autism, and a 7-year-old boy with learning difficulties illustrating the importance of friendship (Merrick, 2014, pp. 46–47).

> I didn't have any friends there, no one to talk to.
> Playing with your friends is nice, cos they play with you.

Others wanting to 'play' with you is understood as a sign of peer acceptance and status, and is important to children. Gallagher, Murphy, Conway, and Perry (2019) interviewed children aged 10–13 years with developmental language disorder (DLD) about their ideal speech and language therapy service and school support. These children expressed their wish for social inclusion, 'so they will want to play with me' (p. 233). As we will hear in Chapter 4, it is not uncommon

DOI: 10.4324/9781003201717-3

for children with SLCN to experience being bullied. Below are the comments from two 10-year-old boys with speech disorder (Merrick, 2014, pp. 42–43)

> There's one of the people in my class bees horrible to me, because when we were on residential he punched me in the eye.
> Because I had some speech problems. They just say it's bad names.

We know from research that children desire better treatment of each other. Interactions in lessons are important, and their comments reveal this. They appreciate the chance to talk to each other in lessons; they find this less exposing and less potentially humiliating than answering teachers' questions in front of the class (Gallagher et al., 2019).

The concept of normality presents a paradox for children with communication difficulties. On the one hand, they have a desire to fit in socially, to have the same friendship opportunities and to celebrate what they have in common with others. This makes them feel 'normal'. At the same time, they are pleased and relieved when their needs are accommodated and differences accepted. This makes them feel they can be themselves. The following extracts from interviews highlight these two truths, from a 12-year-old boy with DLD and a 7-year-old boy with speech sound disorder, respectively:

> I want to talk, you know like, talking the way they [peers] do, so they will listen and think I'm interesting.
>
> (Gallagher et al., 2019, p. 235)

> If like um anybody make fun of them, they [*my friends*] just like stick up for me and say, if they forgot they just say 'Remember he got speaking problems'. [. . .] That's what I like about having friends.
>
> (Merrick & Roulstone, 2011, p. 286)

When we talk about communication difficulty as a disorder, we are using an impairment-focused 'medical model'. We are drawing on the analogy of a physical disease, where something has gone wrong. We compare a person's abilities with normal or typical development and describe the differences in terms of deficits. Children are familiar with this way of talking and thinking about communication, but it is not always positive or helpful. Children's 'discourse of impairment', as I call it, is about things being *wrong, weird* and *no good* (Merrick & Roulstone, 2011). For example, below is a comment from an 8-year-old boy with language disorder:

> Sometimes I find hard to remember easy words. I'm not very good at words. Sometimes I try say something but it sometimes gets wrong and I can't say it.
>
> (p. 285)

However, children can switch between different ways of talking and thinking. Importantly, there is a 'discourse of learning', where children see mistake-making as part of a normal process and communication as a teachable, learnable set of skills. Children recognise some words as hard (such as scientific vocabulary), without this reflecting on the competence of the speaker. In a noisy classroom, and/or when people are tired, and also in conversations using the phone or video conferencing, failure to be understood is a common experience. As one 10-year-old-boy with speech and expressive language disorder said, speaking is like spelling and some words are 'tricky':

> I don't really care if they mistake me on that. Cos that don't really matter, do it? You just need to try and learn it.
>
> (Merrick, 2014, p. 56)

There is also a 'discourse of behaviour', where children are agents, the protagonists in their own lives, deciding what they are interested in and how they want to behave. Children have said that the biggest help is when support is 'tailored' – relevant to their experiences, pitched at the right level for them and, importantly, allowing them to follow their interests.

Types of communication difficulty

We expect to be able to communicate and interact effectively; it feels normal. We expect children's speech and language proficiency to unfold over time, and it usually does. The majority of children in their school years master the rules of conversation; they choose what to say and perfect their timing; they make themselves understood and follow what's going on. Language is a tool that they use to think, to learn and to forge relationships. Every aspect of their social environment provides an opportunity to learn. Meanwhile, almost every part of their developing nervous systems is involved in some aspect of communication, from tone of voice to word finding, from processing sounds to understanding meaning, from articulating sounds to sequencing ideas. It is such a highly adapted and complex system, there are many ways in which, for some children, it can and does go wrong.

As we saw in Chapter 1, more than 1.4 million children and young people in the United Kingdom have SLCN (ICAN, 2018). DLD is one of the most common disorders of childhood and affects children from all backgrounds (Law, McBean, & Rush, 2011; Norbury et al., 2016). DLD is characterised by 'persistent difficulties in the acquisition, understanding, production or use of language that cause significant limitations in the individual's ability to communicate' (ICD-11, 6A01.2). Those children who reach school age with evident language problems are likely to find that the gap between them and their typically developing peers does not close (Rice & Hoffman, 2015). DLD encompasses a variety of problems. Difficulties with expressive language can occur in the presence or absence of receptive language difficulties, speech difficulties, learning difficulties and anxiety disorders

(Dockrell, Norbury, Tomblin, & Bishop, 2008). The thing that they have in common is that some element of communication difficulty doesn't go away. It persists into adulthood.

Five times less common than DLD but perhaps more widely understood, or at least more widely discussed, are *autism spectrum conditions* (also called *autism spectrum disorders*). The prevalence of these conditions in the United Kingdom, including children whose difficulties have not been diagnosed, is estimated at 1.57% (Baron-Cohen et al., 2009). Children with autism spectrum conditions have social and communication difficulties along with strong narrow interests and/or repetitive and stereotyped behaviour. Conditions include *Asperger syndrome*, where language develops at the typical age and cognitive ability is average or above, and *childhood autism*, which is accompanied by language delay and sometimes intellectual disability. Autistic traits are continuously distributed in the population, but diagnosis is only appropriate if these significantly interfere with daily life.

Pragmatic impairment is something that some, but not all, children with SLCN have in common. It's a term often subsumed by 'social communication difficulty'. It can be a problem in its own right, or explained by speech and language limitations (McTear, 1991). A child can have good language skills but still have pragmatic impairment (Volden & Phillips, 2010). A child can also have pragmatic impairment without autism, since autism also involves restricted and repetitive behaviours and interests (Gibson, Adams, Lockton, & Green, 2013). To interact effectively, we need the capacity to express ourselves intelligibly and understand words and sentences accurately. However, in addition to this, there is the element of coordination with our conversational partner(s). Like waltzing or playing ensemble music, language in use is composite. The product is more than the sum of its parts (Clark, 1996). Grice wrote about the conversational 'rules' that are shared by participants in an exchange; the purpose and direction of talk are negotiated (Grice, 1975).

Developments in neuroscience have deepened our understanding of processes operating on an automatic level to support interaction. Eye gaze, response times and small body movements function in sophisticated and coordinated ways to help us synchronise and attune ourselves to others. Not all children are able to deduce, learn or follow 'unwritten' conversational rules, and they can feel excluded as a result (Gallagher et al., 2019). The processes that help us to synchronise with others do not function the same in all children (Pexman et al., 2011; Schilbach et al., 2013).

Pragmatics is defined as language *in use*. It is distinct from, though dependent upon, other linguistic skills, such as articulation, word finding and grammar. Cordier and colleagues (2019) explored the construct of pragmatic language by developing a measure to identify distinct levels of skill among children. Their Pragmatics Observational Measure (POM-2) was designed to look specifically at what is happening during conversation and play with a typically developing partner. Items on the scale are grouped as five elements: introduction and responsiveness; non-verbal communication; social-emotional attunement; executive function, that is, paying attention, planning and organising; and negotiation. The authors have demonstrated the utility of the POM-2 in distinguishing between children. It seems that some children can be reliably identified as having specific difficulty in these areas. However, a focus on pragmatics as a set of skills pertaining to the individual risks overlooking two factors: observer judgement and the part played by the partner.

Because social rules and functions of language vary according to the situation and its participants, the concept of pragmatics is heavily dependent upon judgements of what is *appropriate*. This raises the issue of power and voice: who it is that lays down the norms about what is appropriate, drawing upon what insights and with what assumptions. Assessment judgements tend to be made by adults who, by definition, are outsiders in peer-to-peer interaction. For example, the *Clinical Evaluation of Language Fundamentals* (Semel, Wiig, & Secord, 2017) *Pragmatics Profile* subtest relies on an informant who knows the student to rate the frequency of skills and behaviours, which they consider to be '*culturally appropriate*', '*typical*', '*relevant*', '*correct*' and '*according to the situation*'.

The notion of these judgements building up a profile of the child is problematic, not least because meaning is constructed within the interaction and a matter of cultural perspective (Garte, 2020). Children's willingness to keep on track, to listen and respond, to initiate ideas and assert themselves is related at least in part to the responsiveness and encouragement they receive from their listener. The Children's Communication Checklist (CCC-2) (Bishop, 2003) asks a familiar adult to rate how well children communicate in everyday settings. Items on the scale include '*is babied, teased or bullied by other children*' and '*is left out of joint activities by other children*'. Thus, being rejected by others will reduce your score.

This discourse of interaction as a matter of personal skill is widely available to children, however. A 10-year-old told me he wanted to improve his disordered speech so that he didn't get bullied when he went to secondary school. Many parents link the problem of their child's social exclusion with what they see as the child's own lack of knowledge and competence. Below are the words of a parent of a child with language disorder:

> they are not in the clique – in the gang, they are outsiders and don't know how to get in – they need to know how to get in.
>
> (Gallagher et al., 2019, p. 10)

Some children are considered to have a speech sound disorder. If the percentage of consonants correct is low, this affects intelligibility (Bowen, 2009). The children are often working hard to communicate, and listeners have to listen hard to decipher. Intelligibility is affected by the child's competence as a speaker and the complexity of the what they are saying and also by contextual factors affecting the perception of what they say – these include background noise, whether there are supporting visual cues and how familiar the listener is with the language, the dialect and the person (McLeod, Harrison, & McCormack, 2012). Siblings sometimes understand the child better than less familiar listeners and take on an interpreting role (Barr, McLeod, & Daniel, 2008). For children with speech sound disorders, this can add to the perception that communication breakdown is as much attributable to the quality of partners' listening and attention as to their own speech clarity (McCormack, McLeod, McAllister, & Harrison, 2010).

We have seen in this section how all partners have a role in effective communication. It is unhelpful to put the onus solely on the child with a perceived deficit to acquire new skills, when communicative partners can and do make helpful adjustments to steer conversation, support expression and boost mutual understanding.

Social skills programmes

When we consider the experiences of children with SLCN, we can see that group situations often bring potential difficulties to the fore. These include:

- failure to be understood;
- being quiet or unresponsive; or
- talking excessively without listening to the partner;
- failure to understand; and
- being unable to repair conversation.

The next section reviews some of the most popular social skills programmes designed for use in school to specifically address social difficulties experienced by children with SLCN. In fact, there is a severe lack of research-based interventions for children with SLCN. Law et al. (2012) surveyed clinical practice in the United Kingdom and examined interventions that had been tested in trials. Their report revealed that only 5% of speech and language therapy interventions had a strong evidence base. In this field, it is also worth bearing in mind that *systematic research* is only one of three elements contributing to evidence-based practice: the others are *clinical expertise* and *client preferences* (Dollaghan, 2007). There can be a discrepancy between the functional outcomes and positive experiences that are valued by children and their parents and the evidence gathered in practice and measured in research (Roulstone, 2015). Clinicians are always likely to need to be eclectic in their approach to providing support which is meaningful as well as effective. Case examples – coherent stories about individual people – maintain the crucial element of humanity that can be lost when generalisations and theories are generated (Billig, 2019).

Social skills programmes have generally been developed on the premise that a child must fulfil a certain set of behaviours to be considered normal, and that for children who have a deficit in this area, learning to do so is a desired outcome. Some materials are highly prescriptive. Programmes use modelling and reinforcement to teach children how they should talk and behave in certain situations. Other programmes are more open-ended, training children to think for themselves within a social context, in order to make their own judgements and learn to solve communication problems.

Talkabout (Kelly, 1996, 2018; Wareham & Kelly, 2020) is a social communication skills package presenting a hierarchy of social skills, including sections on self-awareness and self-esteem, body language, conversational skills, friendship skills and assertiveness. The idea is that when these core skills do not come easily to people, they can be taught through activities and games. Kelly aims for people to progress through social skills to social competence, that is, where quality of the interaction is judged positively by others.

Stories are a form of modelling and a way of teaching social mores. Teachers and parents alike make use of true stories and fiction books to highlight things to learn about the world and the way that communication works. In many cultures, children tell true and confabulated stories to each other and through this gain consensus about acceptable interaction and behaviour. From some stories, children abstract rules for themselves; if they struggle with this, the moral can be underlined by others. In the *Social Use of Language Programme* (Rinaldi, 1992, 1995), cartoon monsters depict what can happen when you do or don't use eye contact, listen, take turns, and make appropriate use of space and voice. To consolidate the points in the stories, the programme uses an adult model to get children to judge communication behaviours, and children practise skills themselves through games and activities.

It is one thing to know a social rule because you have been told or shown or learned it from a story (such as *listen* or *take turns*), and quite another to implement the skill in practice. One of the main challenges to the success of social skills programmes is the need to generalise beyond the programme setting. The *Social Use of Language Programme* aims to teach basic skills, role play them in scenarios and for children to then carry out real-life assignments. In practice, there is concern about the considerable step from role play to real life (Constable, 1993).

Social Thinking (Winner & Crooke, 2009) is based on a model of good communication (Winner, 2002) made up of the skills of initiating, listening, understanding abstract language, understanding others' perspectives, Gestalt processing ('getting the big picture') and humour/human relatedness. Each of these variables has been identified as an area of relative weakness for some children who have 'social-cognitive deficits'. The approach to teaching is one of problem-solving (e.g. teaching children to 'read the situation' and take a 'smart guess'), but it is also prescriptive. Social Thinking has generated some oddly phrased 'hidden rules' to teach children, such as 'Think with your eyes', meaning pay visual attention, and 'Listen with your heart', meaning exercise empathy. It uses cartoon examples to teach children what the 'expected' behaviours are in particular situations.

Talkabout, *Social Use of Language* and *Social Thinking* all to some degree take a prescriptive approach, teaching children the social rules we live by. For example, one resource from *Social Thinking* teaches, 'When you behave in a way which is unexpected, it makes people feel uncomfortable' (Hendrix, Palmer, Tarshis, & Winner, 2016). This is certainly not true in all situations, however. When we interact with someone, we can see what they mean and accommodate to them without communication breakdown, even if they depart from 'expected' (typical) social behaviour, and indeed there are comic and creative benefits to the unexpected. This exemplifies the inherent weakness in prescriptive approaches, which fail to take into account the active role that all the partners play in the social construction of meaning. Teaching concrete and specific rules may make them easy for children to understand, but there is little point if they are limited in their application. We are closer to children's social reality if we acknowledge that key areas of interaction involve matters of judgement, balancing two ends of a bipolar scale. Eye contact, for example, is complex and nuanced – too little eye contact and we miss information and signal disinterest, but a lot of eye contact can be disconcerting or even intimidating for others. Willingness to be influenced positively by others may seem to be a good thing, but too much of this can lead to excessive conformity, passivity and lack of creativity. Exercising empathy can be useful, but so too is knowing your own emotional boundaries. Ultimately, what is appropriate or socially helpful is negotiated by participants in the interaction.

From a young age, children become concerned with matters of fairness, justice and the welfare of others. This sense of morality is different to simply knowing group rules and conventions. Children construct moral principles in the course of their experiences and interactions (Piaget, 1932). Morality involves understanding *why* transgressing a rule would be wrong. Morality exists as one domain alongside social knowledge about what people do and expect, and knowledge about what you personally would like. Children are learning to weigh all these up – the *moral*, the *societal* and the *psychological* reasons for how to behave (Killen & Rutland, 2011).

Social Stories (Gray & Garand, 1993) offers flexibility because it provides a template for writing your own stories. The adult chooses scenarios that will be familiar to the child and writes a story to support interpretation of what is said, done, thought and felt. It is written in a way that makes the abstract more concrete and provides an example to follow. Authors of the *Social Stories* method were seeking to address the symptoms of autism, which they understood in terms of difficulties with social cognition, so the stories aim to describe social situations including people's thoughts and feelings in terms of socially relevant cues and define expected responses. They have been described as 'a *visitor's guide* to our social culture', explaining social conventions, their rationale and what is expected (Attwood, 2000, p. 91; emphasis as in original).

Some programmes aim to get children interacting with their peers. Lego® is an intrinsically motivating toy for some children, and *Lego® therapy* (LeGoff, 2017) is a peer-based intervention first designed to coach children with autism in social communication, and extended to children with social anxiety and depression. Interaction is supported by roles (e.g. one child describes the instructions, one finds the correct pieces, one puts them together) and ground rules (e.g. 'Build things together' and 'Keep hands and feet to yourself'), but when difficulties occur, children are encouraged to become aware and solve the problems themselves. The adult coaches the children to mediate the rules and self-regulate, for example, saying 'Hey guys, is someone in here breaking a rule?' (LeGoff, Krauss, & Levin, 2012, p. 230). Lego therapy has been effective with primary schoolchildren with high-functioning autism and Asperger syndrome in reducing autistic symptoms in the areas of social interaction and behaviour (Owens, Granader, Humphrey, & Baron-Cohen, 2008).

While they are motivating and popular, the activities involved in Lego therapy have little in common with tasks that occur in educational settings, where the parameters of peer interaction may well be quite different. Once again, the issue is how easily sustained and applied the skills may be after the end of the intervention in everyday interactions. Some long-term gains have been found in social interaction (LeGoff & Sherman, 2006). An essential feature of Lego therapy, once children are motivated to engage in the sessions, is the 'spontaneous and natural' opportunities for social communication, problem-solving and conflict resolution with peers (LeGoff et al., 2012, p. 234). These open-ended interactions with peers may be the key to the generalisation of social skills from these sessions to other contexts.

Where social skills programmes require children to work in groups, these are usually targeted groups supporting children who all share a SEN. It is less usual to include their typically developing peers. A teacher grouping a child with communication difficulties in interaction with peers may be thinking in terms of providing a good role model and also improving the child's environment, as children learn how best to accommodate and support them (Attwood, 2000). However, there are also benefits to the peers themselves. The experience can combat stereotypes. They can learn to get on with people who are different from them and learn from the challenges that people face.

Active Listening for Active Learning (Johnson & Player, 2009) is a programme which aims to raise children's awareness of their own listening and comprehension skills and behaviours. Children with comprehension difficulties are taught to monitor their own understanding, for example, by identifying which words they know and understand, and when to seek support for something they don't understand. This is based on a principle that using self-monitoring strategies in class will enable more independent learning (Dollaghan & Kaston, 1986). This is an important issue between peers. Children who are able to ask specific questions (such as, 'How did you get 29?') get thoughtful responses, but questions that are too vague or general (such as, 'I don't get it', 'How do you do this?') get low-level help or are ignored (Webb & Mastergeorge, 2003).

However, an important issue for children with poor comprehension may be constructing and managing a positive social identity, not only their functional understanding. These children may feel social pressure to mask their difficulties. Children make social judgements about others in their class, forming perceptions about who tends to request help, who tends to give it, who tends to be silent and what that means about competence (Howe, 2010). Taking responsibility for repairing difficulty requires confidence and social risk as well as awareness, and may be an unfair expectation to put on a child. The conversational partner or teacher also has a responsibility to monitor and respond to the needs of their listener. From the child's point of view, the experience of poor comprehension or indeed poor listening is likely to be, in part at least, a problem attributable to the subject or the speaker. This was the case for the following girls, aged 10 and 11 years, respectively (Merrick, 2014):

> My . . . worst subject is science . . . The words we have to say like *solids*, *opaque* and stuff like that, cos I can't remember all of them.
> Even I just doze off because it's boring, they should make it more fun to listen.

Being included

A unique aspect of inclusive teamwork is its holistic perspective. While the aforementioned programmes assume that problems can be alleviated by focusing on a deficit within the individual, inclusive teamwork is about communication as a collective responsibility. Rather than having a narrow focus on individual function, it has been well-recognised for some time that we should consider communication disability in children holistically (McLeod & Threats, 2008). Inclusive teamwork offers children the chance to be themselves, to be in a supportive environment, and to enjoy effective communication and experience participation.

Inclusive teamwork offers dual cognitive and social benefits for older primary schoolchildren across the board (Howe et al., 2007; Tolmie et al., 2010). Researchers have worked with teachers and mainstream schoolchildren and demonstrated that collaborative group working can be promoted through intervention (Baines, Blatchford, & Kutnick, 2017). Evaluation of the *Social Pedagogic Research into Groupwork* (SPRinG) project demonstrated a significant positive effect on children's interaction, behaviour and the quality of their talk (Baines, Rubie-Davies, & Blatchford, 2009). The integration of children with SEN into group work, however, poses an ongoing challenge. Collaborative settings are demanding for these children, particularly those with SLCN; they become left out or are supported separately by an adult outside of the process (Baines, Blatchford, & Webster, 2015).

Between the ages of 7 and 14 years, dialogue and collaboration become key tools in cognitive and social development (Howe, 2010). However, we know from longitudinal studies that spontaneous improvement in rate of language development is unlikely, and difficulties with peer interaction typically become increasingly marked (Mok, Pickles, Durkin, & Conti-Ramsden, 2014; Rice & Hoffman, 2015). Group intervention tailored to the needs of children with SLCN will, in many cases, be required before these children are equipped to participate in everyday interactive learning.

I carried out a public consultation about inclusive teamwork through a children and young people's health advisory group and through social clubs for children with communication difficulties. For young people, the marginalisation of people with communication difficulties is a live concern. They feel all children should understand communication disorder as 'something normal and common' and that interacting through inclusive teamwork is a way to achieve this. The children and young people consulted saw it as a good thing if, during the programme, communication is 'incidental' to activity and no child feels 'in the spotlight'. They believed sharing common interests with a partner is important, and where groupings take this into account, there is more potential for a 'social bond' to develop. Those with communication difficulties saw inclusive teamwork as potentially fun and leading to desired longer-term outcomes ('You might make friends'). Parents told me that they highly value social cohesion, communication skills and the ability to adapt to others. They see the value of children 'socialising each other' across ability levels, this being natural, effective and enjoyable. There is considerable consensus that developing the patience and empathy to talk to children with communication difficulties is important and beneficial to all parties.

References

Attwood, T. (2000). Strategies for improving the social integration of children with Asperger syndrome. *Autism: The International Journal of Research and Practice, 4*(1), 85–100. https://doi.org/10.1177/1362361300004001006

Baines, E., Blatchford, P., & Kutnick, P. (2017). *Promoting effective group work in the primary classroom: A handbook for teachers and practitioners* (2nd ed.). Abingdon: Routledge.

Baines, E., Blatchford, P., & Webster, R. (2015). The challenges of implementing group work in primary school classrooms and including pupils with special educational needs. *Education 3–13, 43*(1), 15–29. https://doi.org/10.1080/03004279.2015.961689

Baines, E., Rubie-Davies, C., & Blatchford, P. (2009). Improving pupil group work interaction and dialogue in primary classrooms: Results from a year-long intervention study. *Cambridge Journal of Education, 39*(1), 95–117. https://doi.org/10.1080/03057640802701960

Baron-Cohen, S., Scott, F. J., Allison, C., Williams, J., Bolton, P., Matthews, F. E., & Brayne, C. (2009). Prevalence of autism-spectrum conditions: UK school-based population study. *British Journal of Psychiatry, 194*(6), 500–509. https://doi.org/10.1192/bjp.bp.108.059345

Barr, J., McLeod, S., & Daniel, G. (2008). Siblings of children with speech impairments: Cavalry on the hill. *Language, Speech and Hearing Services in Schools, 39*(1), 21–32.

Billig, M. (2019). *More examples, less theory: Historical studies of writing psychology.* Cambridge: Cambridge University Press.

Bishop, D. V. (2003). *The Children's Communication Checklist: CCC-2.* London: Pearson.

Bowen, C. (Ed.). (2009). *Children's speech sound disorders.* Chichester: Wiley.

Clark, H. H. (1996). *Using language.* Cambridge: Cambridge University Press.

Constable, A. (1993). Book reviews: Social use of language programme Wendy Rinaldi Windsor: NFER-Nelson, 1992. Manual. *Child Language Teaching and Therapy, 9*(2), 163–164. https://doi.org/10.1177/026565909300900210

Cordier, R., Munro, N., Wilkes-Gillan, S., Speyer, R., Parsons, L., & Joosten, A. (2019). Applying Item Response Theory (IRT) modeling to an observational measure of childhood pragmatics: The Pragmatics Observational Measure-2. *Frontiers in Psychology, 10*(408). https://doi.org/10.3389/fpsyg.2019.00408

Dockrell, J., Norbury, C., Tomblin, J. B., & Bishop, D. V. M. (Eds.). (2008). *Understanding developmental language disorders in children: From theory to practice.* Hove, East Sussex: Psychology Press.

Dollaghan, C. A. (2007). *The handbook for evidence-based practice in communication disorders.* Baltimore: Paul H. Brookes.

Dollaghan, C. A., & Kaston, N. (1986). A comprehension monitoring program for language-impaired children. *Journal of Speech and Hearing Disorders, 51*(3), 264–271. https://doi.org/10.1044/jshd.5103.264

Gallagher, A. L., Murphy, C.-A., Conway, P. F., & Perry, A. (2019). Engaging multiple stakeholders to improve speech and language therapy services in schools: An appreciative inquiry-based study. *BMC Health Services Research, 19*(1), 226–217. https://doi.org/10.1186/s12913-019-4051-z

Garte, R. (2020). Collaborative competence during preschooler's peer interactions: Considering multiple levels of context within classrooms. *Integrative Psychological and Behavioral Science, 54*(1), 30–51. https://doi.org/10.1007/s12124-019-09496-1

Gibson, J., Adams, C., Lockton, E., & Green, J. (2013). Social communication disorder outside autism? A diagnostic classification approach to delineating pragmatic language impairment, high functioning autism and specific language impairment. *Journal of Child Psychology and Psychiatry, 54*(11), 1186–1197. https://doi.org/10.1111/jcpp.12079

Gray, C. A., & Garand, J. D. (1993). Social stories: Improving responses of students with autism with accurate social information. *Focus on Autistic Behavior, 8*(1), 1–10.

Grice, H. P. (1975). Logic and conversation. In P. Cole & J. Morgan (Eds.), *Syntax and semantics* (Vol. 3, Speech Acts, pp. 41–58). New York: Academic Press.

Hendrix, R., Palmer, K. Z., Tarshis, N., & Winner, M. G. (2016). *We thinkers: Social problem solvers*. Santa Clara, CA: Think Social Publishing Inc.

Howe, C. (2010). *Peer groups and children's development*. Oxford: Blackwell.

Howe, C., Tolmie, A., Thurston, A., Topping, K., Christie, D., Livingston, K., . . . & Donaldson, C. (2007). Group work in elementary science: Towards organisational principles for supporting pupil learning. *Learning and Instruction, 17*(5), 549–563. https://doi.org/10.1016/j.learninstruc.2007.09.004

ICAN. (2018). *Bercow: Ten years on: An independent review of provision for children and young people with speech, language and communication needs in England*. London: ICAN.

Johnson, M., & Player, C. (2009). *Active listening for active learning: A mainstream resource to promote understanding, participation and personalised learning in the classroom*. Stafford: QEd.

Kelly, A. (1996). *Talkabout: A social communication skills package*. Bicester: Winslow Press.

Kelly, A. (2018). *Talkabout for children: Developing self awareness and self esteem* (2nd ed.). Abingdon, Oxon: Routledge.

Killen, M., & Rutland, A. (2011). *Children and social exclusion: Morality, prejudice, and group identity*. Chichester, West Sussex: Wiley-Blackwell.

Law, J., Lee, W., Roulstone, S., Wren, Y., Zeng, B., & Lindsay, G. (2012). *'What works': Interventions for children and young people with speech, language and communication needs*. London: DFE-RR247-BCRP10.

Law, J., McBean, K., & Rush, R. (2011). Communincation skills in a population of primary school-aged children raised in an area of pronounced social disadvantage. *International Journal of Language & Communication Disorders, 46*(6), 657–664.

LeGoff, D. B. (2017). *How Lego-based therapy for autism works: Landing on my planet*. London: Jessica Kingsley.

LeGoff, D. B., Krauss, G., & Levin, S. A. (2012). Lego®-based play therapy for autistic spectrum children. In A. A. Drewes & C. E. Schaefer (Eds.), *School-based play therapy* (2nd ed., pp. 219–235). London: Wiley.

LeGoff, D. B., & Sherman, M. (2006). Long-term outcome of social skills intervention based on interactive Lego© play. *Autism: The International Journal of Research and Practice, 10*(4), 317–329. https://doi.org/10.1177/1362361306064403

McCormack, J., McLeod, S., McAllister, L., & Harrison, L. J. (2010). My speech problem, your listening problem and my frustration: The experience of living with childhood speech impairment. *Language, Speech and Hearing Services in Schools, 41*, 379–392.

McLeod, S., Harrison, L. J., & McCormack, J. (2012). The intelligibility in context scale: Validity and reliability of a subjective rating measure. *Journal of Speech, Language, and Hearing Research, 55*(2), 648–656. https://doi.org/10.1044/1092-4388(2011/10-0130)

McLeod, S., & Threats, T. T. (2008). The ICF-CY and children with communication disabilities. *International Journal of Speech-Language Pathology, 10*(1–2), 92–109. https://doi.org/10.1080/17549500701834690

McTear, M. (1991). Is there such a thing as conversational disability. In K. Mogford-Bevan & J. Sadler (Eds.), *Child language disability 2: Semantic and pragmatic difficulties* (pp. 18–42). Clevedon: Multilingual Matters.

Merrick, R. (2014). *Picture me: Children's views of speech, language and communication needs.* Guildford: J&R Press.

Merrick, R., & Roulstone, S. (2011). Children's views of communication and speech-language pathology. *International Journal of Speech-Language Pathology, 13*(4), 281–290. https://doi.org/10.3109/17549507.2011.577809

Mok, P. L. H., Pickles, A., Durkin, K., & Conti-Ramsden, G. (2014). Longitudinal trajectories of peer relations in children with specific language impairment. *Journal of Child Psychology and Psychiatry, 55*(5), 516–527. https://doi.org/10.1111/jcpp.12190

Norbury, C., Gooch, D., Wray, C., Baird, G., Charman, T., Simonoff, E., . . . & Pickles, A. (2016). The impact of nonverbal ability on prevalence and clinical presentation of language disorder: Evidence from a population study. *Journal of Child Psychology and Psychiatry, 57*(11), 1247–1257.

Owens, G., Granader, Y., Humphrey, A., & Baron-Cohen, S. (2008). LEGO® therapy and the social use of language programme: An evaluation of two social skills interventions for children with high functioning autism and Asperger syndrome. *Journal of Autism and Developmental Disorders, 38*(10), 1944–1957.

Pexman, P. M., Rostad, K. R., McMorris, C. A., Climie, E. A., Stowkowy, J., & Glenwright, M. R. (2011). Processing of ironic language in children with high-functioning autism spectrum disorder. *Journal of Autism and Developmental Disorders, 41*(8), 1097–1112. https://doi.org/10.1007/s10803-010-1131-7

Piaget, J. (1932). *The moral judgement of the child.* London: Routledge and Kegan Paul.

Rice, M. L., & Hoffman, L. (2015). Predicting vocabulary growth in children with and without specific language impairment: A longitudinal study from 2;6 to 21 years of age. *Journal of Speech, Language, and Hearing Research, 58*(2), 345–359. https://doi.org/10.1044/2015_JSLHR-L-14-0150

Rinaldi, W. (1992). *Social use of language programme: Enhancing the social communication of children and teenagers with special educational needs manual.* Windsor: NFER-NELSON.

Rinaldi, W. (1995). *Social use of language programme: Primary and pre-school teaching pack* (2nd ed.). Chilworth: Wendy Rinaldi.

Roulstone, S. (2015). Exploring the relationship between client perspectives, clinical expertise and research evidence. *International Journal of Speech-Language Pathology, 17*(3), 211–221. https://doi.org/10.3109/17549507.2015.1016112

Schilbach, L., Timmermans, B., Reddy, V., Costall, A., Bente, G., Schlicht, T., & Vogeley, K. (2013). Toward a second-person neuroscience. *The Behavioral and Brain Sciences, 36*(4), 393–414. https://doi.org/10.1017/s0140525x12000660

Semel, E., Wiig, E., & Secord, W. (2017). *Clinical evaluation of language fundamentals 5UK*. Bloomington, MN: Pearson.

Tolmie, A. K., Topping, K. J., Christie, D., Donaldson, C., Howe, C., Jessiman, E., . . . & Thurston, A. (2010). Social effects of collaborative learning in primary schools. *Learning and Instruction, 20*(3), 177–191. https://doi.org/10.1016/j.learninstruc.2009.01.005

Volden, J., & Phillips, L. (2010). Measuring pragmatic language in speakers with autism spectrum disorders: Comparing the children's communication checklist-2 and the test of pragmatic language. *American Journal of Speech-Language Pathology, 19*(3), 204–212. https://doi.org/10.1044/1058-0360(2010/09-0011)

Wareham, K., & Kelly, A. (2020). *Talkabout theory of mind: Teaching theory of mind to improve social skills and relationships*. London: Routledge.

Webb, N. M., & Mastergeorge, A. M. (2003). The development of students' helping behavior and learning in peer-directed small groups. *Cognition and Instruction, 21*(4), 361–428. https://doi.org/10.1207/s1532690xci2104_2

Winner, M. G. (2002). *Inside out: What makes the person with social-cognitive deficits tick?* (Rev. ed.). London: Jessica Kingsley.

Winner, M. G., & Crooke, P. J. (2009). Social thinking: A developmental treatment approach for students with social learning/social pragmatic challenges. *Perspectives on Language Learning and Education, 16*(2), 62–69.

3   Learning within relationships

This chapter describes the mechanisms by which children learn when they are collaborating with each other. Relationships and good communication are not just desired outcomes but also the tools by which children engage in learning and develop in their thinking. The chapter explores children's capacity to learn from each other; the part that adults can play in preparing them for effective teamwork and coaching them; and makes the case for teamwork which is inclusive of children with communication difficulties. As we saw in the previous chapter, there is a tradition of explicitly teaching children about social skills through stories, through explaining rules and through role play. However, when children are together, they learn through interaction: they imitate, hear each other's opinions and explanations and stimulate each other's creativity.

Learning to think

If we take a sociocultural approach to understanding the learning process, then we see language as a cultural tool, with social interaction as pivotal. In the work of Vygotsky (1978) and his followers, collaboration is central to learning because in the process children *internalise* interpersonal perspectives. Learning takes place within a *zone of proximal development* – between what the child can do independently and what he or she can achieve through interaction with others. Indeed, it is not just interpersonal, it is cultural. Meaning is provided socially and culturally through collective activity at the *inter*mental level; by actively participating in this, the child appropriates and internalises concepts, memories and intentions at the *intra*mental level (Vygotsky, 1962, 1978). In the course of interaction, learning processes are awakened and knowledge is created; thus, interaction mediates learning (de Valanzuela, 2014).

Scaffolding is the process by which someone with more expertise (a teacher or peer who is more able in some aspect) structures a task to facilitate success for the child who is learning (Wood, Bruner, & Ross, 1976). This is a concept familiar to some teachers and parents; schoolchildren may share the notion too, if not the term. Between peers, there may be a mixture of symmetrical and asymmetrical power relations. Children can be the same age, but perceive status differences in

DOI: 10.4324/9781003201717-4

knowledge or competence. When children help peers by explaining, demonstrating, prompting with questions and allowing their partner time to think, this method of teaching and learning is coming into play.

These theories suggest, and indeed, teachers often believe, that the less competent individual has the most to gain from a partnership. There is the possibility of no progress if the partners do not enter into effective verbal reasoning, and of regressive thinking if a confident partner with misconceptions influences the other (Hogan & Tudge, 1999). However, there is plenty of evidence that providing assistance, especially by explaining and elaborating the explanation, is of benefit to the person explaining as well as to the help seeker (Webb, 2009; Webb & Mastergeorge, 2003). Inclusive teamwork is about capturing the potential for learning that peer-to-peer interaction offers.

When power relations are more symmetrical, children still learn from each other. Piaget, in contrast to Vygotsky, was concerned with learning as a process in the mind of each individual, but he recognised the role of others in constructivism. Piaget (1932, 1971) observed that when children collaborate with peers, they *coordinate* and *compare* the opinions of others with their own. *Cognitive disequilibrium* leads the young thinker to *accommodate* the new ideas or develop a new *schema*. The experience of collaboration helps children to develop their personality too, as they learn to adjust their behaviour to the needs of others and pursue mutual goals (Sullivan, 1953). From middle childhood onwards, peers make comparisons with each other, and there is strong theoretical support that this is an essential trigger for growth (Howe, 2010). In fact, Howe observed that there are benefits to children being exposed to each other's contrasting opinions, even if they do not resolve their differences, as they show superior thinking a few weeks later. It can be a helpful strategy for teacher *not* to effect closure on a discussion at the end of group work, as this allows children the chance to engage in what Howe calls *post group reprocessing*.

Kites rise highest against the wind, not with it.

(Winston Churchill)

Children engage in reasoned argument, compare and resolve difference. As we have seen, there is no doubt from a developmental perspective that children's social participation is vital for their cognitive development, and that interaction with peers plays an important role. Piaget and Vygotsky offered contrasting accounts of child development, yet both these developmental theorists saw the link between mutual peer relations and cognitive-based learning (Kutnick & Berdondini, 2009).

Learning to talk

To learn language, children need varied and rich linguistic input. The same seems to apply for learners with SLCN, but they need more time and more exposure to natural language models than typically developing children (Alt, Meyers, & Ancharski, 2012). If children do not have good levels of social participation, they will be receiving fewer opportunities to learn. Increasing opportunities for participation, for successful communication (and for being challenged) offers the potential to improve speech and language development.

In linguistics, early models of language acquisition focused on language learning as an internal mental process. Chomsky (1965) put forward the theory of the language acquisition device, an innate mechanism in the mind which might make sense of grammar. However, clearly, learning to talk is a collaborative exercise. Bruner (1981) emphasised the role of the adult in supporting children's language development. This was a valuable shift in approach. Analysis of parent–child interaction reveals how both parties are actively involved in driving language development through language use. Efforts to communicate, including mistakes, repairs and responses, play a central role in the process of acquiring words and syntax (Clark, 2014). Parents and caregivers are not the only source of this kind of interaction, particularly as the child gets older. Bronfenbrenner's (1979) model locates the developing child at the centre of a whole system of environmental influences.

Hoff (2006) provided an overview of the way in which social contexts shape and influence children's language development. To learn language, children need two things: a language model (obviously) but also opportunities for communicative experience (mutual engagement and motivation to acquire the language). Mothers support language growth if they are responsive to what their child is doing and pick up on their child's utterances, recasting or expanding on what they say. It is noteworthy that watching the other's behaviour is as important as replying to their speech, because these are all factors in establishing joint attention, which enriches the communicative experience. Peers make a unique contribution to children's language learning experience. We can see in the case of bilingual children that competence in a language is helped by having peers who are native speakers.

Having the chance to actively talk, not just passively listen, contributes in an important way to expressive language development (Ribot, Hoff, & Burridge, 2018). Learning language is an exercise in social coordination, and one in which typically developing children are actively engaged. As Baldwin and Meyer (2007) neatly summarise, three factors in language acquisition are social:

- social *input* (people coordinate their utterances with a point of reference that they share with the child, and vary the intonation and complexity of what they are saying to make it appropriate for the child to understand);
- social *responsiveness* (the child pays attention, tunes in to what others are referring to and gives a reaction; being good at establishing joint attention helps children learn language quicker); and
- social *understanding* (the child is making active sense of what they are hearing and what people are meaning; children 'skilfully mine their social surroundings for clues' (p. 101) to discover meaning).

A child's utterances need a certain level of intelligibility before a conversational partner can respond; this is a problem in the case of some children with SLCN, because that responsiveness is requisite in driving language acquisition

(Conti-Ramsden, 1994). Intelligibility is boosted by familiarity between speaker and listener, and also by contextual support, such as concurrent events or materials to make reference to. When a teacher partners a child with someone they feel will be a good 'role model', they may be thinking more in terms of that person's ability to model language or behaviour. However, to support language development, equally important are the child's interactive skills in tailoring input, problem-solving intelligibility issues, making meaning explicit and attuning their responses.

Learning to get on

We have seen how children learn to think through reasoned discussion with each other, and acquire language competence through interaction. However, they also learn to get on with each other, and this is another dimension to teamwork. Children do not necessarily enjoy working in groups at school. They can feel insecure or threatened, withdraw, turn off-task or look to the teacher (Baines, Blatchford, & Kutnick, 2008). One boy told me he prefers to work on his own, because his partner invariably doesn't do enough work and interrupts him. It is when there are good relations within the group that children are motivated to continue. To a degree, trusting, respectful relationships are a prerequisite for productive group activity; at the same time, better communication and better relations can be *outcomes* of working cooperatively (Gillies & Ashman, 2003).

Theory in social psychology helps us to interpret some of the factors involved in children's motivation to work cooperatively. Deutsch (2012) drew the distinction between *cooperative* and *competitive* behaviours. He first developed *social interdependence theory* in 1949. According to this theory, how goals are structured determines whether people's efforts are cooperative, competitive or individualistic. If goals are *positively interdependent*, then the partners 'sink and swim together' (p. 279), and this is the context for cooperative interaction. We are willing to be helpful to someone whose actions are helpful to us. Deutsch explained this in terms of *substitutability* (when someone else can help us with something, fulfilling our needs) and *inducibility* (the readiness to either accept or reject influence).

Deutsch gave the name *cathexis* to the inborn tendency to react positively towards stimuli that are beneficial and negatively towards those that are harmful. Cathexis gives rise to the potential for love and hate, cooperation and competition. We will view it negatively when a teammate *bungles* (that is, worsens their chances of achieving their goal) if our goals are *positively interdependent* and that person is in a position to potentially fulfil our needs. Conversely, we will view it negatively if an opponent acts *effectively* (that is, improves their chances of achieving their goal) when our goals are *negatively interdependent*, and their success in effect harms our own chances.

These theories explain why setting children up to work collaboratively will involve choosing the task carefully, so that group members perceive everyone working to achieve a joint goal (Johnson & Johnson, 2005). However, teachers have found that simply presenting mutual learning goals does not necessarily create this perception. It is also important to structure individual accountability, so that children have a sense of responsibility to the group, otherwise they can leave themselves or others out. Feelings of responsibility and accountability are going to prevent children from free riding on the efforts of others. The more liked and respected each group member is, the more responsibility they will feel towards the other group members. Liking is complex; we don't necessarily like those better who perform better. Low-achieving peers are chosen as partners just as much as high-achieving ones, and it seems that liking may be based on perceived effort rather than goal achievement. Teachers can make children feel accountable to the group by giving roles and by teaching specific cooperative skills. Johnson & Johnson argue that the effectiveness of a group's efforts to cooperate over the long term depend upon participants taking the time to reflect, identifying and solving the problems they have in working together.

It will be natural to do a task independently (that is, without seeking collaboration) if you know you have everything you need. An experiment with adults showed that people are less likely to be interested in cooperation with the group, even in solving a shared problem, if they have adequate resources to be self-reliant (Gross, Veistola, De Dreu, & Van Dijk, 2020). A task is more likely to be tackled collaboratively if there is a distribution of skills and/or resources across participants.

To work together cooperatively, children need to overcome prejudices that might stem from perceived status differences, gender preferences or understandings of ethnicity (Kutnick & Berdondini, 2009). According to Allport's (1954) *intergroup contact hypothesis*, contact with people reduces prejudice under certain conditions, and these conditions include working towards common goals (Pettigrew & Tropp, 2006). Unfortunately, the reality in many classrooms is that compared to children without support needs, children who have SEN experience significantly fewer opportunities for meaningful social contact with peers (Pinto, Baines, & Bakopoulou, 2019). Contact with someone with communication difficulty can invoke anxiety and discomfort, particularly for people who lack familiarity with the person and with the condition. Anxiety is a negative factor in the link between contact and prejudice. Not only does contact need to be facilitated, but anxiety needs to be minimised. Young people have told me that inclusive teamwork reduces anxiety by having 'a chilled feel', creating a safe context for fun and for mistakes.

We have identified two positive cycles. To work together well, children need to be free from prejudice, and at the same time, prejudice is reduced by working together well. To be trusted group members, children with communication disorders need to communicate effectively, and to do that it helps if they are trusted group members. To break into these cycles, we need to understand children's capacity for motivation and change.

Tyler (2011) theorised that people are motivated to cooperate for broadly two reasons, drawing a distinction between *instrumental* motivation and *social* motivation. He argued that the two sources of motivation are linked but theoretically dissociable. *Instrumental* motivation is where an individual cooperates with the group because there are incentives to do so (or sanctions for not doing). There is a desire to maximise one's own gains, whether short term or long term. In the case of children during school activities, the incentives might be praise or reward from a supervising teacher, or personally desired benefits from success on the group task. *Social* motivation for cooperation, by contrast, is about the intrinsic satisfaction of feeling loyalty, helping people, enjoying your role and achieving something together. This kind of satisfaction influences people even in the absence of any other incentives. People comply with rules that they feel have legitimacy, accept procedures that they feel are fair and ultimately have moral principles which give rise to feelings of responsibility towards others. Cooperation with a valued group supports a positive social identity, feeling proud of being included and respected for one's status within it.

Relations may begin as *task-oriented*, that is, team members are working together for utilitarian reasons, treating each other as interchangeable and getting what they can out of the situation (Deutsch, 2012). They may at the start be instrumentally motivated. However, it appears that through positive contacts, *social-emotional* relations form, that is, team members begin to respond to particular feelings about the people they are with. Importantly for inclusive teamwork, pupils have said that they appreciate and enjoy working in mixed-attainment groups, and their reasons have been primarily about being able to both help and be helped by others (Francis, Taylor, & Tereshchenko, 2020). Children become keen to nurture relationships which are an end in themselves and motivating for their own sake (Tyler, 2011). This means that teamwork does not, at the beginning, require friendship. Friendships are forged by the process of contact and engagement in cooperative interactions.

Children care about who is in their group, how secure they feel, and how supportive, able and likeable they believe others to be. Fostering trusting respectful relationships between pupils and supporting them to work collaboratively is a goal that many teachers will be willing to set, because it is a foundation for a cohesive classroom and a conducive learning environment. Teachers and researchers involved in the SPRinG project took this as a premise in what they called a *relational approach* to learning (Kutnick, Blatchford, Baines, & Tolmie, 2014). The project had positive outcomes in terms of group dialogue, pupil behaviour and achievement. When teachers prioritised positive peer relationships, success or failure of the group was not dependent upon the personalities involved nor at the mercy of interpersonal conflict. Pupils demonstrated enhanced development in relational attitude. Relational training across an academic year had a positive spiral effect on communication and engagement in class (Kutnick & Berdondini, 2009). Importantly, enhanced relational skills were also associated with greater attainment (Baines et al., 2008).

It is a paradox that focusing on collaboration can in the end have greater benefits for children's friendships than focusing on friendship per se. Initially, children are likely to prefer to interact with a familiar trusted friend if they have one. Designated someone else, they have, in my experience, sometimes felt and expressed anxiety, disappointment, annoyance, even outrage. Ten-year-old Aaron, for example, was directed to 'be caring and helpful' with Grant, and complained, 'But I don't care about him'. Twelve-year-old Jason pointed out that in order to interact at all with a partner, it was good to know something about them and have at least one thing in common with them. If an adult is in the position of directing a child to work with a new partner, it can be reassuring to clarify that they are required to work together rather than 'be friends'. In my experience, partnership on time-limited specific educational tasks, with the right support, leads to enjoyment and, over time, the basis of good relations outside of class.

Parsons, Cordier, Munro, and Joosten (2020) found that typically developing playmates aged 6–11 years made gains on the POM-2 as a result of participating in an intervention with children with autism. The implications are relevant for inclusive teaching. The POM-2 was developed for its diagnostic value, and yet progress on component items is observable among unimpaired children. It would be interesting to explore the extent to which gains were valued by the children and other stakeholders. Results suggest that play holds pragmatic challenges and learning opportunities for all children, including those that have already reached or surpassed the benchmark for age-appropriate skills. Intervention for communication has the potential to be an enrichment activity.

Children's relationship development is helped by keeping groups stable in composition. With time and the right guidance, children can get to know each other and learn to trust and respect each other. Baines and colleagues (2008) saw this as good preparation for effective communication and organisation. In the case of children with communication difficulties, however, it could be that effective communication is necessary in order to build the trust, since difficulties with mutual comprehension are a potential barrier to the formation of relationships.

Sadly and ironically, children with SLCN currently routinely miss out on the potential benefits associated with high-quality peer interaction: peers fail to involve them; teachers have concerns about managing group work with them (Baines, Blatchford, & Webster, 2015); even speech and language therapists suggest that conversational work is of limited benefit until language difficulties are 'directly addressed' (Godfrey, Pring, & Gascoigne, 2005, p. 258). They can be stuck in a chicken-and-egg cycle of disadvantage, where they need speech and language skills to participate, but need to participate to make gains in speech and language. Caring relationships are the vitamin C of communication. They are not like medicine, prescribed only for a minority. They are good for everyone, they build resilience and they especially benefit those whose existing levels are critically low.

The role of the teacher

As children interact in pairs and groups over time, they form group norms. The teacher has a leadership role, being explicit about what is valued and to be rewarded. The teacher is also working to enable group norms to emerge and operate from the bottom up. Children develop a sense of fairness early in life. As they mature, their moral judgement emerges out of social interactions, as they learn about the feelings, thoughts and motivations of others (Killen & Rutland, 2011). Inclusive teamwork creates a way for children to explore their own identities without undermining other people's or being undermined. Children and adolescents are active in understanding similarity and difference and constructing identity (Eaude, 2020). The teacher has a role in guiding children to recognise and respect difference and value diversity.

Simply placing pupils in groups does not mean that teamwork will occur. The teacher needs to plan, structure and support teamwork, for a number of reasons (Kutnick & Manson, 1998). First, there are different modes of interaction in class (Howe, 2010). When the teacher takes the lead, engaging in dialogue which essentially follows a sequence of *initiation, response* and *feedback*, then pupils are in *performance* mode, either giving their answers in front of the teacher or being an audience. Below is a classic example (Coulthard, 1977, p. 103):

TEACHER: Those letters have special names. Do you know what it is? What name do we give to these letters?
PUPIL: Vowels.
TEACHER: They're vowels aren't they?

In contrast, when children share ideas in a group, they are in *cooperative* mode. Pupils will not automatically understand the mode of interaction which is appropriate and expected. Second, children sometimes lose interest instead of staying on task, leave the work to others or pull back through concern that they don't want to do it all, instead of everyone combining their efforts. Third, some children have identified impairments which will affect their relationships. These include SLCN and social, emotional and mental health needs.

The teacher can address these concerns and pre-empt problems by the way they brief the children, select the task and debrief the children afterwards. These are discussed in turn below.

Briefing the children effectively means establishing the task and the ground rules in a way that all the children can understand. All members of the group need to understand the common goal and share a sense of purpose. Preparation involves highlighting the cooperative behaviours that you are looking for. At this stage, the teacher can also refigure relationships and influence children's perceived status. It is possible to 'change students' expectations about each other's capabilities' (Webb, 2009, p. 6). It could be that the teacher draws attention to the diversity of abilities involved in the task, encouraging each pupil to formulate a mixed set of expectations, leaving room to fully value the contributions of others (Cohen, Lotan, Scarloss, & Arellano, 1999).

For productive teamwork, the teacher needs to *select a task* where an element of teamwork and effective communication is intrinsic to the success of the activity. A well-presented task minimises the need for adult intervention. While the children are engaged in group work, the adult role should be one of guiding and monitoring rather than controlling (Howe et al., 2007). It could be that the teacher says nothing, unless there is a profound difficulty, such as no interaction, unresolved conflict or persistent domination of the group. If a teacher leaves pupils to it, at least at first, they engage in more collaboration and take more group responsibility (Galton & Williamson, 1992). When teachers observe and monitor cooperative learning rather than making too quick a response, there are benefits to students' thinking (Ding, Li, Piccolo, & Kulm, 2007); they can then guide the students in a more prolonged engagement; this is harder for teachers who need to monitor a number of groups at the same time.

Following an activity, the teacher should *debrief* by encouraging reflection and giving feedback. The objective of the debrief is to encourage change in relation to the target skills, driven by the children themselves. To what extent was the goal of the activity achieved? What was the quality of the cooperation? Some authors argue that in order to get the most educational value out of group work, the children need some 'meta-awareness', because it is helpful to discuss and reflect on how to use talk for sharing ideas and solving problems (Mercer, Hennessy, & Warwick, 2019). However, many children, particularly those with SLCN, will need support in developing this level of awareness and reflection. This is discussed further in Chapter 5.

Worley's (2019) reflections on the role of the teacher are interesting and relevant to teamwork. He has written about teaching philosophy in school where the aim is for children to share a natural diversity of ideas without turning to the teacher for the right answer. He suggested that teaching philosophy is 'an ego-suppressing exercise', and that 'like a good waiter, a good facilitator is present but hidden' (p. 22) during the discussion itself. It may be that intervention is necessary. For example, a group may perceive one member as lower in social and/or academic status and fail to seek or acknowledge that person's participation. The group's low expectations of that individual are in danger of being self-fulfilling. If the teacher is able to be an astute observer, he/she can highlight the value of that child's input, assigning to the individual competence which is specific and relevant to the group. This can equalise participation and reduce the effect of status on behaviour within the group (Cohen et al., 1999). I find minimal prompts can be enough, such as 'Hunter's got a point, did you hear that?', or 'I can see what Wyatt's doing, now there's an idea'.

How far does the teacher's role overlap with that of a therapist? Knowledge and skills in speech and language therapy are highly relevant to the role of a teacher and vice versa. Language is the tool of teachers' trade, and if there is a problem with communication, there is a problem with teaching and learning. If a group of children is working well as a team, there is a foundation for effective learning and a high level of achievement. Because of this, teachers have a vested interest in supporting children's communication. More contentious is whether a teacher's relationship with their pupils can and should ever be a therapeutic one. If so, inclusive teamwork offers a way of infusing everyday teaching practice with effective communication therapy. There is cost pressure on public sector agencies (Beecham, Law, Zeng, & Lindsay, 2012). Many teachers are face-to-face with children in contexts where demand for direct speech and language therapy exceeds supply. In my experience, with motivation and adequate support for their professional development, teachers skilfully and often naturally demonstrate patterns of interaction with their pupils in common with speech and language therapists, psychologists and counsellors: They utilise reflection as a tool, taking a role in supporting the children's own understandings and insights. They explore children's feelings as well as thoughts, link them to their actions, and formulate problems and solutions.

The relationships between children and teachers at school affect intellectual and emotional growth (Baker, Bridger, Terry, & Winsor, 1997). Emphasis on evidence-based practice in teaching and therapy has provided a focus on outcomes, but has led also to an oversight. Research questions explore the impact of particular programmes. What works? While this is positive, it can lead some to over-estimate programme content as a factor, and under-estimate the importance of person-specific relationships that provide the context for the programmes. Talking to children and young people, what comes across strongly is not so much the techniques or programmes in use, but the people involved – the person presenting the programme and the pupils that they are doing it with. It is not only important to know *what* has worked, but with *whom*. Children tell us that it matters who their teacher is, and who is with them in their group.

References

Allport, G. W. (1954). *The nature of prejudice*. Reading, MA: Addison-Wesley.

Alt, M., Meyers, C., & Ancharski, A. (2012). Using principles of learning to inform language therapy design for children with specific language impairment. *International Journal of Language & Communication Disorders*, *47*(5), 487–498. https://doi.org/10.1111/j.1460-6984.2012.00169.x

Baines, E., Blatchford, P., & Kutnick, P. (2008). Pupil grouping for learning: Developing a social pedagogy of the classroom. In R. M. Gillies, A. F. Ashman, & J. Terwel (Eds.), *The teacher's role in implementing cooperative learning in the classroom* (pp. 53–72). New York: Springer-Verlag.

Baines, E., Blatchford, P., & Webster, R. (2015). The challenges of implementing group work in primary school classrooms and including pupils with special educational needs. *Education 3–13*, *43*(1), 15–29. https://doi.org/10.1080/03004279.2015.961689

Baker, J. A., Bridger, R., Terry, T., & Winsor, A. (1997). Schools as caring communities: A relational approach to school reform. *School Psychology Review, 26*(4), 586–602. https://doi.org/10.1080/02796015.1997.12085888

Baldwin, D., & Meyer, M. (2007). How inherently social is language? In E. Hoff & M. Shatz (Eds.), *Blackwell handbook of language development* (pp. 87–106). Chichester: Wiley Blackwell.

Beecham, J., Law, J., Zeng, B., & Lindsay, G. (2012). Costing children's speech, language and communication interventions. *International Journal of Language & Communication Disorders*, *47*(5), 477–486. https://doi.org/10.1111/j.1460-6984.2012.00157.x

Bronfenbrenner, U. (1979). *The ecology of human development: Experiments by nature and design*. Cambridge, MA: Harvard University Press.

Bruner, J. S. (1981). The social context of language acquisition. *Language and Communication, 1*, 155–178.

Chomsky, N. (1965). *Aspects of the theory of syntax*. Cambridge, MA: Massachusetts Institute of Technology.

Clark, E. V. (2014). Pragmatics in acquisition. *Journal of Child Language, 41*(S1), 105–116. https://doi.org/10.1017/S0305000914000117

Cohen, E. G., Lotan, R. A., Scarloss, B. R., & Arellano, A. R. (1999). Complex instruction: Equity in cooperative learning classrooms. *Theory Into Practice, 38*(2), 80–86.

Conti-Ramsden, G. (1994). Language interaction with atypical language learners. In C. Gallaway & B. J. Richards (Eds.), *Input and interaction in language acquisition* (pp. 183–196). Cambridge: Cambridge University Press.

Coulthard, M. (1977). *An introduction to discourse analysis/Malcolm Coulthard*. London: Longman.

Deutsch, M. (2012). A theory of cooperation – Competition and beyond. In E. T. Higgins, A. W. Kruglanski, & P. A. M. van Lange (Eds.), *Handbook of theories of social psychology. Volume II* (pp. 275–294). Los Angeles, CA: SAGE.

de Valanzuela, J. (2014). Sociocultural views of learning. In L. Florian (Ed.), *The SAGE handbook of special education* (Vol. 2, pp. 299–314). London: Sage.

Ding, M., Li, X., Piccolo, D., & Kulm, G. (2007). Teacher interventions in cooperative-learning mathematics classes. *The Journal of Educational Research (Washington, D.C.)*, 100(3), 162–175. https://doi.org/10.3200/joer.100.3.162-175

Eaude, T. (2020). *Identity, culture and belonging: Educating young children for a changing world* (1st ed.). London: Bloomsbury Academic.

Francis, B., Taylor, B., & Tereshchenko, A. (2020). *Reassessing 'ability' grouping: Improving practice for equity and attainment*. Abingdon, Oxon: Routledge.

Galton, M. J., & Williamson, J. (1992). *Group work in the primary classroom*. London: Routledge.

Gillies, R. M., & Ashman, A. F. (2003). An historical review of the use of groups to promote socialization and learning. In R. M. Gillies & A. F. Ashman (Eds.), *Co-operative learning: The social and intellectual outcomes of learning in groups* (pp. 1–18). London: Routledge.

Godfrey, J., Pring, T., & Gascoigne, M. (2005). Developing children's conversational skills in mainstream schools: An evaluation of group therapy. *Child Language Teaching and Therapy*, 21(3), 251–261. https://doi.org/10.1191/0265659005ct291oa

Gross, J., Veistola, S., De Dreu, C. K. W., & Van Dijk, E. (2020). Self-reliance crowds out group cooperation and increases wealth inequality. *Nature Communications*, 11(1), 5161. https://doi.org/10.1038/s41467-020-18896-6

Hoff, E. (2006). How social contexts support and shape language development. *Developmental Review*, 26, 55–88.

Hogan, D. M., & Tudge, J. R. (1999). Implications of Vygotsky's theory for peer learning. In A. M. O'Donnell & A. King (Eds.), *Cognitive perspectives on peer learning* (pp. 37–54). Mahwah, NJ: Routledge.

Howe, C. (2010). *Peer groups and children's development*. Oxford: Blackwell.

Howe, C., Tolmie, A., Thurston, A., Topping, K., Christie, D., Livingston, K., . . . & Donaldson, C. (2007). Group work in elementary science: Towards organisational principles for supporting pupil learning. *Learning and Instruction*, 17(5), 549–563. https://doi.org/10.1016/j.learninstruc.2007.09.004

Johnson, D. W., & Johnson, R. T. (2005). New developments in social interdependence theory. *Genetic, Social, and General Psychology Monographs*, 131(4), 285–358. https://doi.org/10.3200/mono.131.4.285-358

Killen, M., & Rutland, A. (2011). *Children and social exclusion: Morality, prejudice, and group identity*. Chichester, West Sussex: Wiley-Blackwell.

Kutnick, P., & Berdondini, L. (2009). Can the enhancement of group working in classrooms provide a basis for effective communication in support of school-based cognitive achievement in classrooms of young learners? *Cambridge Journal of Education*, 39(1), 71–94. https://doi.org/10.1080/03057640902836880

Kutnick, P., Blatchford, P., Baines, E., & Tolmie, A. (2014). *Effective group work in primary school classrooms: The SPRinG approach*. London: Springer.

Kutnick, P., & Manson, I. (1998). Social life in the classroom: Towards a relational concept of social skills for use in the classroom. In A. Campbell & S. Muncer (Eds.), *The social child* (pp. 165–188). Hove: Psychology Press.

Mercer, N., Hennessy, S., & Warwick, P. (2019). Dialogue, thinking together and digital technology in the classroom: Some educational implications of a continuing line of inquiry. *International Journal of Educational Research, 97,* 187–199. https://doi.org/10.1016/j.ijer.2017.08.007

Parsons, L., Cordier, R., Munro, N., & Joosten, A. (2020). Peer's pragmatic language outcomes following a peer-mediated intervention for children with autism: A randomised controlled trial. *Research in Developmental Disabilities, 99,* 103591. https://doi.org/10.1016/j.ridd.2020.103591

Pettigrew, T. F., & Tropp, L. R. (2006). A meta-analytic test of intergroup contact theory. *Journal of Personality and Social Psychology, 90*(5), 751–783. https://doi.org/10.1037/0022-3514.90.5.751

Piaget, J. (1932). *The moral judgement of the child.* London: Routledge and Kegan Paul.

Piaget, J. (1971). *The science of education.* London: Routledge & Kegan Paul.

Pinto, C., Baines, E., & Bakopoulou, I. (2019). The peer relations of pupils with special educational needs in mainstream primary schools: The importance of meaningful contact and interaction with peers. *British Journal of Educational Psychology, 89*(4), 818–837. https://doi.org/10.1111/bjep.12262

Ribot, K. M., Hoff, E., & Burridge, A. (2018). Language use contributes to expressive language growth: Evidence from bilingual children. *Child Development, 89*(3), 929–940. https://doi.org/10.1111/cdev.12770

Sullivan, H. S. (1953). *The interpersonal theory of psychiatry.* London: Tavistock Publications.

Tyler, T. R. (2011). Motivational models. In *Why people cooperate* (pp. 27–48). Princeton, NJ: Princeton University Press.

Vygotsky, L. S. (1962). *Thought and language.* Cambridge, MA: MIT Press.

Vygotsky, L. S. (1978). *Mind in society.* Cambridge, MA: Harvard University Press.

Webb, N. M. (2009). The teacher's role in promoting collaborative dialogue in the classroom. *British Journal of Educational Psychology, 79*(1), 1–28. https://doi.org/10.1348/000709908x380772

Webb, N. M., & Mastergeorge, A. M. (2003). The development of students' helping behavior and learning in peer-directed small groups. *Cognition and Instruction, 21*(4), 361–428. https://doi.org/10.1207/s1532690xci2104_2

Wood, D., Bruner, J. S., & Ross, G. (1976). The role of tutoring in problem solving. *Journal of Psychology and Psychiatry, 17*(2), 89–100.

Worley, P. (2019). *The if machine: 30 lesson plans for teaching philosophy* (2nd ed.). London: Bloomsbury Education.

4 Mental health and experiences of participation

This chapter examines children's outcomes (mental health and social and emotional adjustment) and the central role played by communication. Social connectedness is a fundamental human need, and we are motivated by a desire for positive interactions with others. It is common for children with communication difficulty to be subjected to marginalisation and victimisation. SLCN are associated with a decline in well-being and quality of life over time. Evidence for the association between language disorder and poor mental health and social and emotional outcomes is particularly strong. Nevertheless, children with communication difficulty can enjoy the benefits of social interaction and friendship, and there is evidence that this has the potential to mitigate the risks for them of poor psychosocial outcomes. A model is presented, where participation is crucial to our definition of health and functioning. The legitimacy of teachers' role in improving children's interaction is discussed.

Social connectedness

Our social environment affects our thoughts and our feelings, and has the power to influence our well-being. Humans are strongly motivated by a fundamental need to belong (Baumeister & Leary, 1995). We naturally seek positive interactions with others and desire to form and maintain interpersonal attachments. Social connectedness is strongly linked to psychological health, and it is a protective factor against the ill effects of victimisation (Liu, Carney, Kim, Hazler, & Guo, 2020).

Sadly, it is less common for children with SLCN to experience social inclusion and connectedness than for some other children. Communication difficulties are associated with social difficulties, particularly as children get older. Schoolchildren with DLD are at risk of marginalisation and victimisation (Conti-Ramsden & Botting, 2004). Among children aged 7–8, those with language disorder were four times more likely to report elevated levels of bullying than typically developing peers (Redmond, 2011). Problems with peer relations typically become more marked in these children over time (Mok, Pickles, Durkin, & Conti-Ramsden, 2014). The extent to which we are socially included or excluded predicts how we feel about ourselves. For children who are victimised (not only those with SLCN),

DOI: 10.4324/9781003201717-5

the risk is enhanced of internalising problems, anxiety, depression, withdrawal and loneliness (Liu et al., 2020).

Marginalisation is multifaceted. Children experience inclusion and marginalisation in different ways. Messiou (2006) gave examples of children who, when interviewed, seemed to be experiencing marginalisation, but classmates did not view the situation in the same way. I have certainly worked with well-liked but depressed teenagers with SLCN who care deeply about their friendships and perceive peer rejection. Equally, there were children who appeared to be in marginalised situations without feeling it. Some children, particularly those with externalising behaviours, are controversial – highly liked by some and rejected by others.

There are some naturally occurring reasons why children socially exclude others, and these need to be understood. Children may exclude others in anticipation or expectation of negative behaviours (e.g. not listening to someone because you don't expect their ideas to be sensible, or not playing with them, because you expect them to be aggressive). Social groups share common goals, and it will seem legitimate and fair to children to exclude someone who causes (or may cause) disruption (Killen & Rutland, 2011). Different forms of reasoning come into play in a friendship situation compared to a larger or more formal group. Children might regard it as 'unfair' to exclude someone from a certain group, but at the same time regard it as a matter of 'personal choice' whom they are friends with. When a child is excluded for legitimate reasons, they are likely to learn something about how to interact with others. When exclusion is for reasons that are unclear or unfair, however, consequences can be highly negative.

Communication difficulty and mental health

It is a statistical truth that children with communication difficulties commonly also have difficulties with emotional and mental health. Of 144 young people referred for mental health treatment, Cohen, Farnia, and Im-Bolter (2013) found that 65 (45%) were affected by some form of language impairment. This was three times greater than for the comparison group. For children and young people with language disorder, this pattern is reflected in findings from longitudinal studies in the United Kingdom, Canada, the United States and Australia. Language disorder in a cohort of 62 English young people predicted shyness and low self-esteem in adulthood (Durkin, Toseeb, Botting, Pickles, & Conti-Ramsden, 2017). Language disorder in children also predicted anxiety and depression in later life (Botting, Toseeb, Pickles, Durkin, & Conti-Ramsden, 2016). A meta-analysis conducted in the United States found that *most* (81%) of the 838 children identified as having emotional and behavioural disorders had communication difficulties, and up to half of these were moderate to severe language disorders (Hollo, Wehby, & Oliver, 2014). Children with language disorder in the United Kingdom are more than five times more likely than their typically developing peers to have poor mental health as adults (Law, Rush, Schoon, & Parsons, 2009); poor receptive language is a significant risk factor for adult mental health and well-being (Schoon, Parsons, Rush,

& Law, 2010). In Canada, Brownlie, Bao, and Beitchman (2016) found that among adults with a history of communication disorder, there were higher rates of social anxiety. Language disorder was associated with a higher probability of having a psychiatric disorder in early adulthood, though not later in life, with maltreatment being a much stronger factor than language disorder (Bao, Brownlie, & Beitchman, 2016). In Australia, children with DLD have reported poorer quality of life than their typically developing peers and a decline in quality of life with age (*n* = 872) (Eadie et al., 2018).

Educational and employment outcomes *can* be good for individuals with DLD. However, compared to controls, this group obtained lower academic and vocational qualifications and on average left education earlier, according to a UK study (Conti-Ramsden, Durkin, Toseeb, Botting, & Pickles, 2017). The majority of juvenile offenders have poor language skills (Bryan, Freer, & Furlong, 2007). A high proportion of young offenders (over 50%) have language disorder, much higher than non-offenders from the same population (Snow & Powell, 2011). Moreover, young offenders with DLD have been found to be more than twice as likely to reoffend within a year of their court order compared to those without DLD (Winstanley, Webb, & Conti-Ramsden, 2020). Thus, the implications of DLD are not confined to childhood (Paul & Norbury, 2018), and indeed, social difficulties and risks of social exclusion become exacerbated over time.

Positive interaction as protective

Despite this catalogue of findings, it is clear that mental health difficulties and poor social outcomes are *not inevitable* for individuals with communication disorders. Relationships are a theme defining quality of life for children and young people with communication disorders (Markham, van Laar, Gibbard, & Dean, 2009). In common with their peers, children with SLCN wish to have identities which are positively evaluated. If their condition has a label, they do not tend to use it, and prefer to emphasise what they have in common with others (Lyons & Roulstone, 2017). Positive relationships are a protective factor for children with DLD, whose well-being is otherwise at risk (Lyons & Roulstone, 2018). Having even just one best friend that really 'gets' you leads to positive self-concept and to developing communication skills. Opportunities for such relationships may depend on attitudes towards inclusion and tackling prejudice and wrong assumptions. Parents of children with communication difficulties highlight the need for more understanding about the difficulty from those around them (Roulstone & Lindsay, 2012).

In early childhood, there is a case for saying that language intervention and teacher practices in the classroom can ameliorate the negative relationship between communication disorder and social, emotional and mental health outcomes. Despite unidentified language difficulties being high among young offenders, Winstanley, Webb, and Conti-Ramsden (2018) found that language disorder that was identified and supported at school was *not* associated with increased contacts with the police later in life. Law, Rush, Clegg, Peters, and Roulstone (2015) found that while children from socially disadvantaged backgrounds are at risk of behaviour difficulties in adolescence, pragmatic skills at age 9 have a mediating effect. Thus, stronger social skills in childhood can reduce the risk of behaviour difficulties in adolescence. Language and behaviour develop together. According to Chow, Cunningham, and Wallace's (2020) interaction-centred model of language and behavioural development, positive relationships, consistent expectations and emotional support provide a context for both language growth and improved behaviour (both of these benefiting academic performance). Drawing on evidence from early years' settings, they recommended proactive positive behaviour support and emphasised the importance of a warm teacher–child relationship.

Thus, there is theory and a weight of evidence that relationships and interactions in childhood are important for later social and emotional adjustment, behaviour and mental health. It is not only relationships with adults, but also relationships with peers that hold this importance. *Friendship support* has been found to be the strongest positive predictor of resilient psychosocial functioning in healthy teenagers (van Harmelen et al., 2017). For children at risk of depression and social anxiety in their teens, supportive friendships are protective (McDonald, Bowker, Rubin, Laursen, & Duchene, 2010). Friendships have a role in preventing adolescent depression for children who have experienced bullying (van Harmelen et al., 2016). Children with communication difficulty may be in a poor position to benefit from these factors. Even among children aged between 3 and 6 years, language competence, especially understanding, has been found to predict peer popularity (Gertner, Rice, & Hadley, 1994). Studies reveal an overall tendency for children with language disorder to reach adolescence with poorer-quality friendships than some other children (Durkin & Conti-Ramsden, 2007).

However, there are children with communication difficulties who enjoy good friendships. In children both with and without communication difficulties, empathy supports friendship quality, and equally, friendship supports empathy in a positive cycle of development (van den Bedem, Willems, Dockrell, van Alphen, & Rieffe, 2019). Toseeb and colleagues have demonstrated that children with communication difficulties can be prosocial – helpful, sharing and comforting towards others. Being prosocial is a strength to encourage and nurture, particularly in middle childhood, because it is protective against social and emotional difficulties (Toseeb & St Clair, 2020). In their analysis of a large cohort of longitudinal data, Toseeb et al. (2020) found that children who had better friendships and more prosocial play at age 7–9 years were less likely to have emotional or behavioural problems at the age of 11 years. That was specifically true for children with language disorders as well as their classmates. The authors suggested that therapeutic intervention for children with language disorders should include opportunities for developing prosocial play, because through such opportunities, children deploy, practise and learn key relationship skills which are protective, particularly against externalising problems.

Unfortunately, such opportunities have, for many children, not been the norm. Webster and Blatchford (2013) observed a common model of support in school where pupils with SEN experienced the 'almost constant accompanying presence' of a teaching assistant, physical separation from others and relative isolation from their peers during day-to-day school life. Pinto, Baines, and Bakopoulou (2019) found that children with SEN and children with externalising and internalising behaviours had lower levels of peer acceptance; but they also found that frequency of meaningful contact with peers played a greater role in peer acceptance than SEN status or behaviour.

As we saw in Chapter 3, participation with others in a collaborative context is a basis for learning to get on. Cooperative efforts tend to promote more positive relationships and greater psychological health than do competitive or individualistic efforts (Johnson & Johnson, 2005, p. 326). What that can mean for children with communication disorders is that coaching and supporting cooperative peer interactions is likely to nurture relationship skills which will be a vital resilience factor in later life.

Participation and health

Participation is a dimension of health, according to the International Classification of Functioning, Disability and Health for Children and Youth (ICF-CY) (World Health Organization, 2007). This replaced an older model that focused on impairment, disability and handicap. It is now well-recognised that our ability to *participate* in activities is as much part of being healthy and functioning well in society as the health of our bodies. This is true for children and adults alike. The biopsychosocial model is the basis for the ICF-CY. According to this model, *body* structures and functions and *health conditions* are not the only components in a person's overall health or disability. Also influential are the *activity* they carry out, the *participation* they experience, and *contextual factors*. The relationship between each of these components is bidirectional. *Activity* and *participation* refer to 'the execution of a task or action' and 'involvement in a life situation'. For children at school, activity and participation might include, for example, speaking, writing messages, communicating in conversation, focusing attention, thinking, learning to read and write, relating with persons in authority, informal relationships with friends and peers, sibling relationships and relationships with parents (McCormack, McLeod, McAllister, & Harrison, 2009). According to the World Health Organization definition, therefore, our participation (including our opportunities for social interaction) and contextual factors (including the way that we are supported and treated by others) are all dimensions of our health and functioning.

Symptoms of communication difficulty can be treated by adaptation of the environment. As we saw in Chapter 1, conversation partner training programmes are effective and common practice in the treatment of adults with aphasia, yet, the role of peers has been overlooked in speech and language therapy service delivery with children. Inclusive teamwork has the potential to be positive for children's participation and thus their health and function. Children's SLCN can be understood as health *or* educational, because indeed they are both. Some teachers may argue that improving children's participation is in itself an educational goal, while others will see improved participation as being a consequence of good inclusive teaching (Watson, Emery, Bayliss, Boushel, & McInnes, 2012). Either way, there is a role for teachers as well as therapists in supporting the participation of children with SLCN.

Teachers cannot, on the whole, legislate for friendships; as children get older, adults (in many cultures) recognise that these are a matter of children's personal choice (Killen & Rutland, 2011). Indeed, somewhat radically, Watson and colleagues (2012) have been critical of schemes such as peer mediation, where children are required to survey each other using rules and language determined and taught by the adults. These authors argued that there was something unjust about adults imposing their own concepts on children's interaction and 'professionally problematising' (p. 138) children's social experiences. In contrast, classroom activities are the domain of the teacher, and teachers' input regarding children's interactions has legitimacy. Inclusive teamwork is proposed to engage children in enjoying and improving peer interaction on specific collaborative tasks. It is hoped that this will impact children's choices outside of the tasks regarding interaction, inclusive behaviours and ultimately friendship, as a spontaneous, not prescribed, progression.

References

Bao, L., Brownlie, E. B., & Beitchman, J. H. (2016). Mental health trajectories from adolescence to adulthood: Language disorder and other childhood and adolescent risk factors. *Development and Psychopathology, 28*(2), 489–504. https://doi.org/10.1017/S0954579415001054

Baumeister, R., & Leary, M. (1995). The need to belong: Desire for interpersonal attachments as a fundamental human motivation. *Psychological Bulletin, 117*, 497–529. doi.org/10.1037/0033-2909.117.3.497

Botting, N., Toseeb, U., Pickles, A., Durkin, K., & Conti-Ramsden, G. (2016). Depression and anxiety change from adolescence to adulthood in individuals with and without language impairment. *PLoS ONE, 11*(7). https://doi.org/10.1371/journal.pone.0156678

Brownlie, E. B., Bao, L., & Beitchman, J. (2016). Childhood language disorder and social anxiety in early adulthood. *Journal of Abnormal Child Psychology, 44*(6), 1061–1070. https://doi.org/10.1007/s10802-015-0097-5

Bryan, K., Freer, J., & Furlong, C. (2007). Language and communication difficulties in juvenile offenders. *International Journal of Language & Communication Disorders, 42*(5), 505–520. https://doi.org/10.1080/13682820601053977

Chow, J. C., Cunningham, J. E., & Wallace, E. S. (2020). Interaction-centered model for language and behavioral development. In T. W. Farmer, M. A. Conroy, E. M. Farmer, & K. S. Sutherland (Eds.), *Handbook of research on emotional and behavioral disorders: Interdisciplinary developmental perspectives on children and youth.* Routledge.

Cohen, N. J., Farnia, F., & Im-Bolter, N. (2013). Higher order language competence and adolescent mental health. *Journal of Child Psychology and Psychiatry, 54*(7), 733–744. https://doi.org/10.1111/jcpp.12060

Conti-Ramsden, G., & Botting, N. (2004). Social difficulties and victimization in children with SLI at 11 years of age. *Journal of Speech, Language and Hearing Research, 47*(1), 145–161.

Conti-Ramsden, G., Durkin, K., Toseeb, U., Botting, N., & Pickles, A. (2017). Education and employment outcomes of young adults with a history of developmental language disorder. *International Journal of Language & Communication Disorders*, *53*(2), 237–255. https://doi.org/10.1111/1460-6984.12338

Durkin, K., & Conti-Ramsden, G. (2007). Language, social behavior, and the quality of friendships in adolescents with and without a history of specific language impairment. *Child Development*, *78*(5), 1441–1457. https://doi.org/10.1111/j.1467-8624.2007.01076.x

Durkin, K., Toseeb, U., Botting, N., Pickles, A., & Conti-Ramsden, G. (2017). Social confidence in early adulthood among young people with and without a history of language impairment. *Journal of Speech, Language, and Hearing Research*, *60*(6), 1635–1647. https://doi.org/10.1044/2017_JSLHR-L-16-0256

Eadie, P., Conway, L., Hallenstein, B., Mensah, F., McKean, C., & Reilly, S. (2018). Quality of life in children with developmental language disorder. *International Journal of Language & Communication Disorders*, *53*(4), 799–810. https://doi.org/10.1111/1460-6984.12385

Gertner, B. L., Rice, M. L., & Hadley, P. A. (1994). Influence of communicative competence on peer preferences in a preschool classroom. *Journal of Speech and Hearing Research*, *37*(4), 913–923.

Hollo, A., Wehby, J. H., & Oliver, R. M. (2014). Unidentified language deficits in children with emotional and behavioral disorders: A meta-analysis. *Exceptional Children*, *80*(2), 169–186. https://doi.org/10.1177/001440291408000203

Johnson, D. W., & Johnson, R. T. (2005). New developments in social interdependence theory. *Genetic, Social, and General Psychology Monographs*, *131*(4), 285–358. https://doi.org/10.3200/mono.131.4.285-358

Killen, M., & Rutland, A. (2011). *Children and social exclusion: Morality, prejudice, and group identity*. Chichester, West Sussex: Wiley-Blackwell.

Law, J., Rush, R., Clegg, J., Peters, T., & Roulstone, S. (2015). The role of pragmatics in mediating the relationship between social disadvantage and adolescent behavior. *Journal of Developmental and Behavioral Pediatrics*, *36*(5), 389–398. ISSN 0196–0206X.

Law, J., Rush, R., Schoon, I., & Parsons, S. (2009). Modeling developmental language difficulties from school entry into adulthood: Literacy, mental health, and employment outcomes. *Journal of Speech Language and Hearing Research*, *52*(6), 1401–1416. https://doi.org/10.1044/1092-4388(2009/08-0142)

Liu, Y., Carney, J. V., Kim, H., Hazler, R. J., & Guo, X. (2020). Victimization and students' psychological well-being: The mediating roles of hope and school connectedness. *Children and Youth Services Review*, *108*, 104674. https://doi.org/10.1016/j.childyouth.2019.104674

Lyons, R., & Roulstone, S. (2017). Labels, identity and narratives in children with primary speech and language impairments. *International Journal of Speech-Language Pathology*, *19*(5), 503–518. https://doi.org/10.1080/17549507.2016.1221455

Lyons, R., & Roulstone, S. (2018). Well-being and resilience in children with speech and language disorders. *Journal of Speech, Language, and Hearing Research*, *61*(2), 324–344. https://doi.org/10.1044/2017_JSLHR-L-16-0391

Markham, C., van Laar, D., Gibbard, D., & Dean, T. (2009). Children with speech, language and communication needs: Their perceptions of their quality of life. *International Journal of Language and Communication Disorders*, *44*(5), 748–768.

McCormack, J., McLeod, S., McAllister, L., & Harrison, L. J. (2009). A systematic review of the association between childhood speech impairment and participation across the lifespan. *International Journal of Speech-Language Pathology*, *11*(2), 155–170. https://doi.org/10.1080/17549500802676859

McDonald, K. L., Bowker, J. C., Rubin, K. H., Laursen, B., & Duchene, M. S. (2010). Interactions between rejection sensitivity and supportive relationships in the prediction of adolescents' internalizing difficulties. *Journal of Youth and Adolescence*, *39*(5), 563–574. https://doi.org/10.1007/s10964-010-9519-4

Messiou, K. (2006). Understanding marginalisation in education: The voice of children. *European Journal of Psychology of Education*, *21*(3), 305–318. Retrieved from www. jstor.org/stable/23421610

Mok, P. L. H., Pickles, A., Durkin, K., & Conti-Ramsden, G. (2014). Longitudinal trajectories of peer relations in children with specific language impairment. *Journal of Child Psychology and Psychiatry*, *55*(5), 516–527. https://doi.org/10.1111/jcpp.12190

Paul, R., & Norbury, C. F. (2018). *Language disorders from infancy through adolescence: Listening, speaking, reading, writing and communicating*. St Louis, MO: Elsevier.

Pinto, C., Baines, E., & Bakopoulou, I. (2019). The peer relations of pupils with special educational needs in mainstream primary schools: The importance of meaningful contact and interaction with peers. *British Journal of Educational Psychology*, *89*(4), 818–837. https://doi.org/10.1111/bjep.12262

Redmond, S. M. (2011). Peer victimization among students with specific language impairment, attention-deficit/hyperactivity disorder, and typical development. *Language, Speech, and Hearing Services in Schools*, *42*(4), 520–535. https://doi.org/10.1044/0161-1461(2011/10-0078)

Roulstone, S., & Lindsay, G. (2012). *The perspectives of children and young people who have speech, language and communication needs, and their parents*. London: DFE-RR247-BCRP7.

Schoon, I., Parsons, S., Rush, R., & Law, J. (2010). Children's language ability and psychosocial development: A 29-year follow-up study. *Pediatrics*, *126*(1), e73–e80. https://doi.org/10.1542/peds.2009-3282

Snow, P. C., & Powell, M. B. (2011). Oral language competence in incarcerated young offenders: Links with offending severity. *International Journal of Speech-Language Pathology*, *13*(6), 480–489. https://doi.org/10.3109/17549507.2011.578661

Toseeb, U., Gibson, J. L., Newbury, D. F., Orlik, W., Durkin, K., Pickles, A., & Conti-Ramsden, G. (2020). Play and prosociality are associated with fewer externalizing problems in children with developmental language disorder: The role of early language and communication environment. *International Journal of Language & Communication Disorders*, *55*(4), 583–602. https://doi.org/10.1111/1460-6984.12541

Toseeb, U., & St Clair, M. C. (2020). Trajectories of prosociality from early to middle childhood in children at risk of developmental language disorder. *Journal of Communication Disorders*, *85*. https://doi.org/10.1016/j.jcomdis.2020.105984

van den Bedem, N. P., Willems, D., Dockrell, J., van Alphen, P. M., & Rieffe, C. (2019). Interrelation between empathy and friendship development during (pre)adolescence and the moderating effect of developmental language disorder: A longitudinal study. *Social Development*, *28*(3), 599–619.

van Harmelen, A.-L., Gibson, J., St Clair, M., Owens, M., Brodbeck, J., Dunn, J., . . . & Goodyer, I. (2016). Friendships and family support reduce subsequent depressive symptoms in at-risk adolescents. *PLoS ONE*, *11*(5), e0153715. https://doi.org/10.1371/journal.pone.0153715

van Harmelen, A.-L., Kievit, R. A., Ioannidis, K., Neufeld, S., Jones, P. B., Bullmore, E., . . . & Goodyer, I. (2017). Adolescent friendships predict later resilient functioning across psychosocial domains in a healthy community cohort. *Psychological Medicine*, *47*(13), 2312–2322. https://doi.org/10.1017/S0033291717000836

Watson, D., Emery, C., Bayliss, P., Boushel, M., & McInnes, K. (2012). *Children's social and emotional wellbeing in schools: A critical perspective.* Bristol: Policy Press.

Webster, R., & Blatchford, P. (2013). *The making a statement project: Final report: A study of the teaching and support experienced by pupils with a statement of special educational needs in mainstream primary schools.* London: The Nuffield Foundation.

Winstanley, M., Webb, R. T., & Conti-Ramsden, G. (2018). More or less likely to offend? Young adults with a history of identified developmental language disorders. *International Journal of Language & Communication Disorders, 53*(2), 256–270. https://doi.org/10.1111/1460-6984.12339

Winstanley, M., Webb, R. T., & Conti-Ramsden, G. (2020). Developmental language disorders and risk of recidivism among young offenders. *Journal of Child Psychology and Psychiatry, 62*(4), 396–403. https://doi.org/10.1111/jcpp.13299

World Health Organization. (2007). *International Classification of Functioning, Disability and Health Children and Youth Version (ICF-CY).* Geneva: WHO.

5   The dimensions of inclusive teamwork

This chapter sets out an analysis of inclusive teamwork in terms of three dimensions: *enjoy, talk* and *achieve*. It explores how these dimensions correspond with models of teamwork from education, speech and language therapy and psychology. It also looks at the way in which children develop awareness of their own inclusive teamwork and the motivation to work well as a team and to improve levels of collaboration.

Is inclusive teamwork about *skill* – abilities that we acquire and apply, or about *behaviour* – actions and efforts that we choose to make? The danger of talking about skill is that it overlooks the role of motivation and children's agency. The risk of talking about behaviour, on the other hand, is that this can be associated with blame rather than support. SLCN are often interpreted in terms of lazy, cheeky or rude behaviour. This is unfair and it is counter-productive if children are simply expected to behave better. Moreover, teamwork and participation are facilitated by behaviours practised across the group as a whole, and should not in all fairness be attributed to the personal contribution of any one individual. Children and young people are continually learning and developing. In the analysis that follows, I outline the dimensions of teamwork, recognising that for the interaction to be positive, children not only acquire inclusive teamwork skills, but are also motivated to employ them and supported in doing so.

Enjoy

What one 10-year-old boy liked most about inclusive teamwork was that 'it's a really nice feeling, it makes you feel good'. Positive emotions affect our thinking, our behaviour and our learning. They are the ideal starting point for interaction and a desirable end point. Thus, the first dimension of inclusive teamwork is establishing and maintaining an enjoyable connection with the other person. For supervising adults, it is easier to recognise the need for such connection than to bring it about. We may find ourselves prompting children to listen, pay attention and respond. These prompts sometimes work and sometimes do not: the process of relating to a partner is complex and hard to legislate. Yet, inclusive teamwork depends upon confirmation, often through non-verbal signals, that there is a mutual

DOI: 10.4324/9781003201717-6

readiness to engage and interact, and partners establish this together. The non-verbal signals that we send out indicate our feelings, our expectations and our intentions. Those signals both stem from and contribute to a feeling of *safety*. When people – children or adults – feel safe and no element of threat, they are more prosocial as well as more creative in their problem-solving (Gilbert, 2005). These are the conditions for trust and mutual respect to germinate and grow.

Reading linguistics as an undergraduate, I was taught about communication as being like a chain of events, comparable to the functions of the transmitter, signal and receiver in broadcasting. The *speech chain* takes us from a speaker's thoughts via an acoustic message to the listener's interpretation (Denes & Pinson, 1973). It's a neat way of analysing the physics and biology of speech and audiology. Each component is inherently separable in the model. If there is a problem with communication, it can reside with the speaker, the signal or the listener. However, communication is much more than transmission of messages, because of its social context and dynamic nature. Indeed, sometimes interaction is *all* about who the participants are and what their relationship is. Eleven-year-old Asmita said of her mother that she was 'really nice, 'she just listens to me' (Merrick, 2009, p. 85). Her simple comment captures the meaning that 'listen' can have.

Psychologists interested in attachment have analysed what is involved when two people interact positively. Specifically looking at caregiving relationships, Kennedy, Landor, and Todd (2011) describe interaction as *attuned* when both partners play an active role and are responsive and harmonious. Video interaction guidance provides a way of promoting attunement through reflection on interactions within a particular relationship, looking at certain key principles in particular (Pomerantz, 2017). I would argue that these principles, and the idea of using video as a tool for reflection, have relevance for children wishing to reflect on and improve peer interaction. First, being *attentive* and *curious* encourages *initiative*, and this is the foundation for attuned interactions. The child needs to feel able (safe, loved, recognised, important) to initiate, whether this be in the form of an action or words. Second, being *responsive*, that is, *receiving* the initiative (e.g. returning eye contact, smiling, nodding) and *replying* is an essential ingredient (indeed, the 'core'); interaction ensues which is enjoyable, each person giving and taking short turns. Finally, the relationship develops by *building* on ideas, making new suggestions and deepening the discussion.

As children develop, they may care about their relationships with others, but not know how to establish and maintain them. Attwood (2000) provided a 'checklist of friendship skills' (p. 92) which included the following:

- providing compliments at appropriate times and knowing how to respond to a compliment;
- distributing conversation and resources equitably;
- recognising when and how to respond with empathy to the other person's circumstances and feelings;
- accepting suggestions and incorporating the ideas of others in the activity;

- showing interest and observing the other person, in order to monitor their contribution to the activity and body language.

In an attempt to address the difficulties faced by children with Asperger syndrome, Attwood advocated teaching children to recognise why these skills are important. He proposed that rewarding children for practising them and giving encouragement to the partner were instrumental in effecting change.

The term *synchrony* has been used by psychologists to describe when people mutually coordinate their attention with sensitivity and reciprocity. In using this term, we are focusing on the way partners harmoniously match each other (e.g. in the pace of their activity and their body posture). In early childhood, the ability to achieve synchrony is crucial for social, emotional and cognitive growth (Harrist & Waugh, 2002). Between preschoolers, shared meaning emerges as they play, often as a result of what they are *doing* with the materials rather than from linguistic exchanges (Garte, 2016). It seems plausible that across age groups, cultures and settings, non-verbal actions have a special role to play in collaborative activity and that synchrony is a useful concept, particularly so in the case of groups that include children with communication disorders.

It is often recommended that group work should involve pupils of similar status, because they will be more likely to share and explain their ideas to each other. Without an equal 'feel' between pupils, those with perceived higher status are likely to dominate. What does this mean for children with SEN? Howe et al. (2007, p. 561) observed that productive interaction between children has the power 'to *create* mutuality and equality' within cross-age groups. Children make assumptions about the knowledge and ability of others, including those who are younger or who have been identified as having SEN, but these assumptions can change as children engross themselves in shared tasks and discover each other's strengths and interests. Moreover, pupils co-construct knowledge with their peers. This blurs the lines between who is providing and who is receiving explanations, and who came up with which idea. For example, an 8-year-old boy with a language disorder was working with a classmate on a construction task. They had been briefed to build a structure from Geomag™ that was strong and stable. The partner with stronger language skills and no identified special needs assumed leadership, issued instructions and was constructing a large cube. The boy with language disorder mirrored his activity but was making a pyramid. He showed this saying 'triangle', and his partner accommodated his good idea. The non-verbal context and synchrony provided a good basis for effective communication and problem-solving.

Educationalists have recognised that for successful teamwork, pupils need to *want to* work together. A relational approach was one of the foundations of the SPRinG project (Kutnick, Blatchford, Baines, & Tolmie, 2014). Teachers carried out whole-class programmes across the academic year, aiming to foster the development of relationships and skills conducive to collaborative group work. One of the key principles of this teaching programme was that groups form and develop over time. To facilitate successful group work, teachers first encourage children to want to work together, building trust and respect. This relational work is the foundation of effective communication (including active listening, explaining and sharing ideas) and more advanced group skills (including planning, organising and reaching consensus). Positive outcomes of this project with older primary schoolchildren were reported not only in terms of the quality of group discussion, but also in terms of pupils' willingness to sustain active participation in a shared task (Baines, Rubie-Davies, & Blatchford, 2009).

If teamwork is inclusive, all members will be contributing in some way. Being left out or feeling that you have nothing to offer can equate to a feeling of social exclusion. It would be simplistic, however, to consider *equal* participation to be the marker of good teamwork. The amount that each child says does not reflect the extent of their role in the interaction. Participation can be non-verbal as well as verbal. A few words can be influential. Even silent observation can actively contribute to the group. The whole group can benefit from a leader who, in stimulating and galvanising others, may take a higher proportion of turns.

Speech and language therapists have analysed participation not just in terms of how frequently children initiate and respond during small group interaction, but also whether turns are *contingent* on those of others and the task. Here, contingency means being responsive with something that is relevant, not being stuck in your own train of thoughts or simply making random remarks. Thiemann and Goldstein (2001) looked at groups that included children aged 6 to 12 years with autism. According to Thiemann & Goldstein, contingent responses included acknowledging, agreeing, answering, responding with a related comment and clarifying (e.g. 'What did you say?'). The scheme proved clinically meaningful, as these measures have shown significant change in response to treatment (Maione & Mirenda, 2006; Thiemann & Goldstein, 2001).

Thus, listening has two stages. The first is to *engage* attention, but the second is to *show* that you have been listening by giving a response which is contingent, following and dependent upon the previous utterance. You want to know what your partner thinks, and you encourage each other to join in by the response that you give. For example, Liam and Alex, both aged 12 years, were debating whether zoos are cruel. They enjoyed the way their ideas built on each other. Alex felt animals should be allowed their wild environment with their families. Liam introduced a point about protecting endangered animals. Alex agreed and talked about the benefits of wildlife reserves. Both boys were talkative, but timed their turns carefully so as to respect and listen to the ideas of their partner.

In the above example, there was agreement and consensus. The perception of similarity and agreement is important to people's sense of liking and affiliation. For this reason, children are sometimes cautious about expressing dissent to their peers. However, rapport is not *dependent* upon two people agreeing or indeed on having anything in common. This is evident from, for example, police work. The principles of rapport are more influential than liking or agreement in establishing connection. This can be helpful when children appear initially to find little in common. Alison and Alison (2020) identified the cornerstones of rapport as honesty, empathy for your partner's beliefs and values, respect for your partner's autonomy and the ability to identify elements that guide a conversation towards a goal.

There are many reasons why children do *not* connect and get on. We should start with listening. Children *want* to listen if they find it interesting, important or fun, more salient than other distractions and if they like the speaker. 'I wasn't listening' does not imply a skill deficit in that area, but rather a choice. Below, a 10-year-old girl with language disorder is talking about listening in a whole-class situation:

> I feel bored, really, in class, really. Like, I just don't concentrate. I just chat.
> (Merrick, 2009, p. 72)

For children who have poor verbal comprehension, listening is going to take a lot of effort and the gains need to feel worth it for them. In a teamwork situation, it helps if there is a non-verbal element to the interaction, if talk is the right level for everyone to understand and if the appeal of the task is high. If a child is initially unresponsive, there are many things that partners do to arouse each other's attention and engage interest – say their partner's name, ask a question or simply watch and wait expectantly. One 9-year-old boy responded only after repeated invitations from his partner, demonstrating the value of patience, warmth and persistence:

SILAS: [making a paper plane] Mm . . . hold the left side. Grant, do *you* wanna join in any?

GRANT: [looking at a book] No.

SILAS: I can't do it all by myself. [3 second pause] We're supposed to . . . It's teamwork. [8 seconds, Silas explores the instructions] So we need to drop the left side to the outside. [Grant looks up and joins in].

Being ignored or teased are potentially among the most annoying and painful experiences of peer interaction. In my experience, children have been disregarded and insulted when their partner has perceived the situation to be competitive rather than cooperative, and/or when they have prejudice. They may believe, for example, that their partner can't talk or doesn't listen, without waiting to try and see. As we saw in Chapter 3, the adult has an important role here, briefing the children, reinforcing the cooperative nature of the task and reflecting with them, highlighting the diversity and value of abilities demonstrated.

While insulting is always hurtful, it would be simplistic to outlaw teasing and ignoring. These *can* have a positive function in collaborative interaction. Children don't hesitate to ignore a bad suggestion, especially if they are able to progress with their own better idea. Not 'listening', that is, noticing but not responding to a partner, has its place in children's interactions. The focus remains on the task, and new ideas emerge. Equally, if a child makes a poor suggestion or an error of judgement, their partner may tease them in a way that has a friendly function. Being playful makes light of mistakes and encourages creativity. The message here is that very few ways of responding are definitely right or wrong. It is all to do with the intended and actual effect that they have on the partner. Inclusive teamwork is about the participants, with adult support, observing and reflecting upon what is happening and what is working.

Children readily go off-task and off-topic. Our emotions and our interest determine the salience of the stimuli around us, and some children have more executive control over their attention than others. Judging children's utterances for their contingency is more complex than is at first apparent, however. What seems appropriate and connected will depend upon the observer's perspective and priorities. For example, if a child breathes in a waft from the next-door canteen and says 'macaroni cheese for lunch', we might judge the comment to be creating an off-task distraction, or alternatively to be contingent on group members' shared experience and valuable for group cohesion.

Poor verbal comprehension is a common reason for children going off-task and off-topic. Sometimes, children with communication disorders take on a joker role to mask or deflect from the lack of contingency that they experience a lot of the time. I would argue that conversational partners have a role in helping each other to stay relevant and not sideline a classmate in this way.

As we saw in Chapter 4, empathy develops alongside friendship, and some children will have better developed skills than others. It is a specific area of difficulty for some children with autistic spectrum disorders. It is also harder for children to feel for others and be interested in them if they are experiencing high levels of stress, anxiety or depression themselves. In inclusive teamwork, children may well fail to pick up on the other's feelings. However, they can be helped by being guided to do so.

Occasionally, children have spoiled a potentially good connection by being too intimate, for example, trying to touch their partner's shoulder or looking more at their partner than the task materials. This may be because they feel desperate for friendship or have a different level of maturity to their partner. Partners sometimes choose to put up with this rather than offend, but they may appreciate adult support to give kind but honest feedback to their partner. As with teaching empathy, feelings and reactions can be pointed out objectively without reproach.

How we communicate is influenced by the mood we are in as well as our personality (*state* as well as *trait*). Negative emotions can affect thinking and behaviour in a self-perpetuating cycle. Some children may be suffering from difficulties with attachment or from social anxiety. Pressure to speak is almost always counter-productive for children suffering from these conditions. However, the creation of a safe interpersonal connection will be supportive and encouraging. It is helpful to highlight here the importance of having shared materials and an open-ended task with non-verbal elements in order to nurture positive and successful interactions.

Selective mutism is an anxiety disorder affecting people's ability to speak in different situations. In treatment, the speech and language therapist will support those interacting with the child to consider what will constitute an anxiety-free environment for the child, and to build from a central comfort zone of trust and rapport (Johnson & Wintgens, 2017). Whenever a child is anxious about talking, it is likely to be helpful to keep the emphasis on participation and to value non-verbal contributions, rather than target speaking per se. Initial small steps towards any kind of participation can lead to more prolonged and in-depth social interaction, particularly if the child is able to progress at a pace they are comfortable with.

Talk

'We talk to each other' is often children's reflection on inclusive teamwork when it is going well. The second dimension of inclusive teamwork is *talking* in the sense of mutually exchanging ideas, information, opinions and maybe feelings. When children are talking well, they are understanding each other's speech, comprehending and expressing themselves and putting ideas together.

Whether because of a speech sound disorder, a quiet voice or background interference, we cannot always catch and understand what others say. In an inclusive team, children monitor and repair conversation, saying when they have not understood, and checking back on their interpretation. Both parties expect mutual understanding, asking, self-correcting and clarifying where necessary. It can be uncomfortable and even embarrassing to ask for repetition, especially more than once, and feigning comprehension or passing over ambiguities feels like the polite thing to do. After all, if you are paying attention, then you are often able to anticipate and guess what someone might be saying. Yet authentic communication is dependent upon accuracy and honesty. A child is not being included if their ideas are only being assumed or misunderstood.

Self-correction is a skill that children typically acquire at the same time as meaningful speech. When intelligibility is disrupted on a regular basis, however, children may be less able or willing to attempt to self-correct. Asking for clarification is a natural process but hard work for children with language disorder (Kamhi, 1987). It is therefore helpful for conversational partners to play an active role. Responsibility for mutual understanding is shared. In their *Active Listening for Active Learning* programme, Johnson and Player (2009) emphasised how children with communication difficulties can benefit from learning to recognise and say when they have not understood, but equally, all participants should be prepared to check their understanding, encourage elaboration and challenge the reasoning of their partners.

It is not unusual for intelligibility to be impaired when communicating via video conference and video call. Interruptions to the audio signal create the need for repetition and checking back. I have noticed that it can be particularly frustrating for children with communication difficulties. At the same time, in creating communication difficulties for all parties, it also levels the playing field and normalises the frequent use of conversational repair strategies.

Partners may not share understanding of the same vocabulary or grammar; too many ideas at once can be hard to process. If someone is not comprehending, they may need to be shown by example and with reference to things you can see and handle. If someone can't find the right word, their listener may be able to suggest one. Partners also share a role in reasoning, imagining and predicting. Children explain their ideas, elaborating with enough detail. It takes confidence to ask specific questions to understand another person's ideas or feelings better.

Particular challenges are faced by children with speech and language disorders. Early in development, all children find it easier to talk about objects and events in the here-and-now with perceptible referents and find it harder to talk about things that are remote in time or conceptually abstract. For various reasons, this same pattern is true even after early childhood for many with communication difficulties. One way of supporting communication is to draw in reference to perceptible referents because this boosts intelligibility. Pictures, objects, diagrams, handling equipment, observing things happen in real time, listening out for sounds, even smelling and tasting, these all become important and valuable when interacting with children with communication difficulties. Below are the words of a 12-year-old boy with language disorder:

> I like experiments it makes it easy to learn if you are doing it. So we did an experiment before with washing up liquid and more art cos you can think about things, it's another, it gives you another way to think about things
> (Gallagher, Murphy, Conway, & Perry, 2019, p. 8)

A developmental hierarchy was developed by Blank, Rose, and Berlin (1978, 2003), outlining four kinds of questions that children between the ages of 3 and 5 can typically answer. These 'levels' of language processing characterised an increasing complexity, from matching verbal and perceptual information ('What's this?') to abstract reasoning ('How do you know that?'). The four levels have intuitive appeal among some speech and language therapists and teachers. The gist of the scheme is that the conversational partner needs to tune in to the language competence of the child. Reasoning is a key feature of exploratory thinking; there are children with language delay or disorder for whom the language required is likely to be particularly challenging, and this makes participation more difficult. Moving down the hierarchy and talking about the things that can be directly perceived is likely to make participation easier for children who appear to be struggling with the language involved.

The simplicity of the above scheme may be seductive, but taking a linear view of development and consulting norms for young children is going to have limited application among schoolchildren with communication disorders. One of the challenges of interacting with a child with SLCN is the unpredictability of their skills. Until they are familiar with each other, partners do not necessarily know what to expect. It can be difficult to gauge what a child understands or is likely to be able to say. Moreover, evident difficulty in one area does not imply limitation in another, since a child can show a complex profile of strengths and weaknesses across a range of component skills. The Clinical Evaluation of Language Fundamentals (CELF 5UK) (Semel, Wiig, & Secord, 2017), an assessment battery commonly used by speech and language therapists, has multiple independently scored subtests. A profile may, for example, contrast auditory comprehension skills with expressive language skills, or contrast measures of semantic development (knowing what things mean) with measures that reflect the ability to interpret and produce sentence structures.

The information to be gained from a professionally administered standardised language assessment can be absolutely key to planning the type of linguistic support from which a child will benefit the most. However, even when this information is available, it is not the whole story, because children in real-life interactions use (or fail to use) their language skills and non-verbal communication in dynamic ways. One of the most important components of inclusive teamwork for children with communication difficulties will be the mutual willingness to check communication – to look for evidence of attention and understanding, to spot breakdowns in communication and repair misunderstanding with clarifications, simplifications or explanations.

Educationalists have long understood that high-quality communication and dialogue leads to high-quality thinking. Good students will be able to ask, challenge and criticise in a constructive way in order to find out more. They will learn the most if they are prepared to question or disagree, give reasons, elaborate, tolerate criticism, concede a good point and incorporate the ideas of others. This assumption underpins a pedagogy of 'dialogic teaching'. There are clear benefits when the teacher asks open-ended, thought-provoking questions, listening to pupils and encouraging them to elaborate their ideas (Alexander, 2017).

These principles have been applied to schoolchildren in groups too. Mercer (1996) recognised that children could learn to work together and think together. The way people talk depends on their relationships and on their interpretation of the situation and its ground rules. From classroom observations of children working in groups, Mercer identified three distinct social modes of thinking, the third being the most educationally useful:

- *disputational* (competitive; individuals making assertions and disagreeing);
- *cumulative* (empathy; uncritically confirming what others say); and
- *exploratory* (constructively critical; engaging with ideas, challenging, justifying and reaching eventual joint agreement).

Littleton and Mercer (2013) demonstrated how teachers can encourage *exploratory thinking* and the academic value that this can have for pupils. *Thinking Together* (Dawes, Mercer, & Wegerif, 2000) was a programme of activities for the teaching of thinking skills through group work. It was written for children aged 8–11 years but not specifically with children with communication difficulties in mind. The programme is based on ground rules, which the authors recommended should be negotiated with the pupils. They acknowledged the importance of respect and encouragement, suggesting 'Everyone in the group should be encouraged to speak by the other members' and 'Contributions are treated with respect'. Beyond this, they proposed several points which they considered would encourage 'effective, reasoned, exploratory talk' (p. 30):

- all relevant information is shared amongst the group;
- assertions and opinions should be backed up by reasons;
- it is important to challenge and discuss suggestions and opinions; and
- alternative options are carefully considered before any decision is made.

All the points are sound in principle. One problem with the idea of negotiating such ground rules with the pupils is that this requires a threshold of communication skills with which some pupils, including those with communication difficulties, may not approach the task in the first instance. It was the view of Dawes and colleagues that ground rules should be 'established' before carrying out further activities. However, the SPRinG programme demonstrated a 'cycle of reflection', with children reflecting and evaluating their group working after each activity. The children learn from experience and as they become more adept, they integrate their learning into more general rules; thus, rules may be the product of experience rather than the starting point (Kutnick et al., 2014). Certainly, in the case of groups that include children with communication difficulties, awareness of rules, understanding of the terminology for talk (explain, reason, respond, persuade, compromise etc.) and appreciation of the importance of communicative functions can sometimes only emerge from the experience of group working.

In reviewing observational studies, Webb (2009) reiterated the educational value of pupils learning to explain and elaborate their ideas. She identified aspects of teamwork instrumental in this. She underlined the basic need to acknowledge and pay attention to each other's ideas, build on these and make connections. Beyond this, children also benefit from sharing knowledge, justifying and clarifying their ideas. Webb gave particular consideration to how children give and receive help. Children readily understand that teamwork involves helping each other. Help, however, has some different meanings. It can mean simply joining in and taking your fair share of the work. Counter-productively, it can also mean doing the task *for* someone (e.g. giving someone the answer). Ideally, as defined by Webb, it means helping someone to elaborate their own understanding by explaining or asking them questions. For classmates playing this role, sometimes a teacher or teaching assistant is the main model, and this tends to position them in an asymmetric power relationship. However, such an imbalance is not inevitable. Children profit from explanations when they are comprehensible and of sufficient detail, and this is why asking good questions is so important for all children.

Achieve

A boy described inclusive teamwork as 'a good way for people to solve a problem'. This third dimension of inclusive teamwork focuses on the achievement of a goal through collaboration, problem-solving and consensus. The process includes organising between you how to approach a complex task, for example, what to do first and adopting or delegating roles. It involves keeping the goal in mind and reminding others so that everyone stays on task and monitoring how you are getting on. Children involved in inclusive teamwork notice the topic shifts that happen in conversation, work out when to stick with a topic and when to move on. They know when to be considerate and when to be decisive. There may be disagreements, and they negotiate, persuade or compromise in order to reach consensus and resolve conflict.

I have not infrequently found that children admit immediate defeat when faced with a problem to solve. For example, when given the components to make a wind-powered car, they have simply said 'I don't know what that is. I don't know what you do'. This depends on attitude perhaps more than ability. *Hope* is a particularly useful concept because it has been found to correlate with life satisfaction and to be a protective factor in young people's development (Liu, Carney, Kim, Hazler, & Guo, 2020). Successful experiences of overcoming obstacles have the potential to teach children to engage in seeking solutions to new problems. Hopefulness is not just a feeling in a particular situation. Children with hope envision ways to attain desired goals and have the sense of agency to act on these (Snyder et al., 1997).

Leaders of business employees are often advised to delegate and define roles when working in teams, for example, chair, facilitator, recorder, sponsor, coach (Parker, 2009). This is supportive of efficiency and successful outputs from the group. Identifying required roles and matching them to participants is, in fact, a high-level skill. In the case of schoolchildren (or indeed, adult employees), a supervising adult can delegate roles to ease the demands of the task, but allowing them to do this themselves enhances the responsibility that the children take for organising themselves.

One of the most challenging aspects of inclusive teamwork and perhaps also the most rewarding is collectively working through a problem where solutions are various, not immediately obvious and ideas differ. Dawes and colleagues (2000) included in their *Thinking Together* programme two ground rules about consensus and decision-making: the group 'should try to reach agreement' and 'accepts collective responsibility for decisions made and actions taken because of those decisions'. Webb (2009) defined the skills involved in reaching consensus and achieving a shared goal: 'recognize and resolve contradictions between their own and other students' perspectives' and 'monitor how the unfolding contributions relate to the goal'. For the authors of the SPRinG project, 'advanced group work-ing skills' were the final step in a developmental sequence after consolidating social and communication skills (Kutnick et al., 2014). Pupils would be presented with challenging tasks that required joint problem-solving skills, not only sharing ideas but also discussing and reaching consensus. Pupils achieved this advanced level of teamwork collectively through experience and reflection as a cohesive group over time.

Forest School is an outdoor learning context in which children work along-side peers on activities to achieve mutual goals. It is an inclusive child-focused approach offering the opportunity to engage in supported risky play. There is a growing awareness of the benefits of Forest School for children's learning and well-being; it has been blended with the traditional curriculum in some schools. Coates and Pimlott-Wilson (2019) invited primary schoolchildren to reflect on their experiences of Forest School and found that the element of collaboration and teamwork contributed to their learning and enjoyment. Children described increas-ing their social networks and learning to resolve conflict. Below are the comments from one 8- or 9-year old girl:

> You've come closer with people from going to Forest School because you had to work in a group with people who might not have been your friends but are now like your best friends! I always think I learn better when I'm with my

friends, but sometimes I can learn a little bit more than I already did about something with someone, like a boy or something.

(p. 33)

Speech and language therapists have identified organisational skills as potential areas of individual deficit. The POM-2 includes *paying attention, planning* and *organising* as items categorised under *executive function* (Cordier et al., 2019). The measure also includes *conflict resolution* under the element of *negotiation*. These are items regarded as having utility in differentially diagnosing pragmatic impairment. There are some children for whom staying on task and seeing how ideas sequence and problems resolve present particular challenges.

Inclusive teamwork can be assessed in a different way to pragmatic skill, however. Responsibility for solving problems is shared across the whole group. The dimensions of teamwork need only be present in the group and not necessarily practised by each member. It only takes one member to

- frame the first step in a task, for example [looking at the electric bulb], 'I really wanna know if this can be on', 'Let's see if this connects';
- direct the others, for example, 'You ask me a question now', 'You need to decide'; and
- recognise when the task is complete, for example, 'We've done it!', 'That's it!'

Sometimes children are convinced that they know best, and come across to their partner as opinionated, snobby, saying no to everything. Among the friendship skills outlined by Attwood (2000) were giving and tolerating criticism and managing disagreement. His belief was that experience and teaching about these things was helpful. Some authors point out that challenging interpersonal experiences are essential drivers of motivation to succeed and persistence in the face of failure (Watson, Emery, Bayliss, Boushel, & McInnes, 2012). However, children often feel that disagreement disrupts connectedness and liking. They may seek to avoid confrontation, and feel angry and threatened when they experience it. One of the most reassuring lessons that can come out of inclusive teamwork for children is the way in which disagreement *need not* disrupt rapport, if they are able to connect, talk things through and stay focused on the shared goal.

Children's awareness of inclusive teamwork

So far, I have outlined the dimensions of inclusive teamwork: enjoy, talk and achieve. For participants to develop in these areas, they need to engage in, reflect on and learn from experience. This section looks at what psychology can tell us about children's awareness of the communication that they are involved in and the extent to which they can (and want to) make changes.

Knowing yourself is no easy matter. People's own ratings of how agreeable they are can be significantly different from those of observers, suggesting that we don't accurately know how we 'come across' (Sun & Vazire, 2019). Moreover, some people find it more difficult than others to use their memories to build self-identity and know their own personality. It could be, for example, that people with autism are less introspective and don't use memory to construct self-identity in the same way as some others (Robinson, Howlin, & Russell, 2017).

Metacognition refers to the capacity to think about and manage one's own cognitive processes. For example, if you see yourself as talkative, if you realise you have not understood something, if you wish you had more information, or if you judge a task to be difficult, these are all types of metacognition, according to the original concept (Flavell, 1979). Speech and language therapy often involves not only helping a child to learn new skills, but teaching them to monitor how and when to use these skills. Therapists administering the *Social Communication Intervention Programme*, for example, engaged children in metacognition by talking about aspects of knowledge, thinking and communication (Gaile & Adams, 2018). Below are some examples:

- Knowledge: 'Do you know what's in my box?'; 'Shall I give you a clue?'; 'I think you worked it out'.
- Steps in the task: 'for this work, we have to think really hard. So you might want to close your eyes and picture it in your head'.
- Strategies to use: 'We can say to ourselves, "Never . . . [Child: "Never mind"].
- Repairing conversation: 'I got a bit lost because I didn't know what you were talking about'.

The study highlights the function of labelling aspects of communication in order to talk about them and thus think about them. The programme is prescriptive; the therapist introduces terms with which the children may be unfamiliar and teaches 'rules' with examples, role playing what happens when they are (and are not) followed.

However, we should also be attuned to picking up on what the children themselves are noticing, and the ways they have of expressing this. For example, a 10-year-old with autism observed a video clip of himself and a partner having what I felt was a good discussion, listening and reasoning adeptly, but he described this as 'He's lying' and 'I proved him wrong'. The appreciation of opinion as fact was posing a barrier to good teamwork, and reflecting on this issue was the key to developing the social bond between them.

When coaching children in inclusive teamwork, it is helpful to have a notion of what will be easiest for them to conceptualise. Perhaps the simplest form of metacognition is knowing *what* you're thinking and doing, for example, 'I was listening', 'We were arguing'. More advanced is evaluating or planning *how* to think about things, for example, 'This is difficult for me, let's do it step-by-step' (Veenman, Van Hout-Wolters, & Afflerbach, 2006). This distinction is between what has been called *metacognitive knowledge* and *metacognitive skilfulness*. Wall (2008) evaluated a programme where teachers were implementing and investigating approaches such as cooperative learning, assessment for learning and thinking skills, and teachers were routinely engaging with pupil views. Some pupils as young as 4 and 5 years old who were participating in that project not only showed that they had metacognitive knowledge, but also could demonstrate metacognitive skilfulness. However, Wall did find that metacognition develops and increases as pupils get older and become more experienced learners, particularly in relation to *skilfulness*, which was associated with reasoning, problem-solving and abstract thinking.

When reflecting with children, it is also important to think about the timing. You experience metacognition *before* an exercise (such as feeling that you are liable to fail), *during* one (such as feeling puzzled or suddenly having an idea) and *after* an exercise (such as evaluating that you did well). It is likely to be easier for children to reflect on their own interaction in the moment, or at least immediately afterwards. Some children proficiently reflect on teamwork and are able to use metacognitive vocabulary. Below are some examples:

> You have to *persevere*.
> We've got to *encourage* each other.
> We were both *taking turns* spinning it.
> We were *talking* to each other, having the *pros and cons*.
> That was *intimidating*.
> It was really like, he's *ignored* me.

Children may be genuinely more aware of others than themselves, and they may pick fault more readily than compliment; it is important to acknowledge feelings (e.g. of frustration) but also preserve a positive ethos of encouragement. If there are complaints and criticisms arise, these need to be handled sensitively, with an emphasis on overcoming difficulties as a team.

Some children draw a blank when asked to evaluate after the interaction has concluded, perhaps because they simply can't remember or are not aware, or vocabulary about mental states is too abstract for them to comprehend and use. Branigan and Donaldson (2019) reported on a school with a commitment to making learning visible and getting children involved in their learning. Teachers were using *structured thinking activities* to encourage retrospective reflection on the learning process, but the authors noticed that a child can become quickly bored by these, giving superficial responses just to please the teacher and being 'silly'. To make metacognition meaningful, I have found it helpful to make the most of awareness *during* the activity for some children. The teacher can make a note of reflections that the children make, such as 'This gives me an idea', 'I've changed my mind' to remind them later and help them label what has been happening. They can also interject with short simple feedback relevant to that moment. Hearing the terminology in context (when the children are *experiencing* inclusive teamwork) helps children to become aware, understand and (crucially) learn to identify and label inclusive teamwork skills for themselves. Below are some examples:

> Listening, good.
> That was a friendly look.

Good question.
You gave your reason, well done.
Very organised.
You know what you're trying to do.

Motivation

As well as metacognitive awareness, children also need motivation to cooperate with each other. As we saw in Chapter 3, according to social interdependence theory, even if participants begin as self-interested, they organise themselves into a cooperative group when they have a common goal, and perceive it as such. This builds on the principles of Gestalt psychology, where the whole is greater than the sum of its parts: a group is a dynamic whole with interdependent members. Here we are talking about the goal of the group members rather than the goal of the task. As Johnson and Johnson (2005) point out, teamwork needs effort to keep it co-operative:

> There is an inherent tendency of cooperation to fail because competitive actions undermine its effectiveness. Effective cooperation requires very active and sustained effort to prevent it from deteriorating into competition.
>
> (p. 297)

Group members look to the actions of others and judge how to perceive the situation. If members coerce or threaten, obstruct the success of another, enhance power differences or try to deceive, then the situation both is perceived as competitive and becomes competitive. The power of a common goal to motivate *cooperative* behaviour depends theoretically upon three processes:

a) each group member sees that another can do something for them and vice versa;
b) members feel positively towards each other as they see the actions of others benefit them; and
c) members are willing to do things for each other.

These processes are enabled when group members get to know and trust each other, communicate accurately, accept and support each other and resolve conflicts constructively. Thus, it is good planning to structure tasks in such a way as to encourage cooperation rather than competition, to make communication essential to the task, not just incidental, and to provide a goal or purpose that all team members can share (Mercer, Hennessy, & Warwick, 2019).

We know from cognitive behavioural therapy that talking about and reflecting on one's own thinking and behaviour can be a tool for change. Techniques have been adapted for use with children and young people. Stallard (2005) proposed a collaborative approach between therapist and child. The therapist does not steer the child towards a preconceived outcome but uses questioning to move in an open-minded way *with* the child through stages of thought. First, the child is supported to identify his or her own thoughts and the feelings and behaviours associated with these, see things that have been overlooked and put information together with increasing objectivity. The child is encouraged to act like a scientist or detective, setting out to discover information and test ideas. Being able to think creatively and re-evaluate (e.g. What sense do you make of this now? Is there another way of thinking about this?) is the last of these stages.

Motivational interviewing is a counselling technique, originally developed to address problems such as addiction (Miller & Rollnick, 2013; Rollnick & Miller, 1995). There is some evidence to suggest that the techniques of motivational interviewing can be effective with children and young people (Snape & Atkinson, 2016). The approach is based on the assumption that motivation for change will come from the client, and responsibility for change resides with him or her. The counsellor is a partner in the process as the client identifies his or her thoughts and feelings, explores their meaning and the connections between them, makes a rational analysis and finally reappraises the situation. It has been used to reflect with children and young people on such areas as their academic achievement and their school-based motivation, and bring about improvement.

However, language competence is a criterion for these types of therapy. Stallard recognised that children may not have the language to volunteer information or to adequately describe their feelings and suggested ways of supporting this visually. Open questions are demanding on expressive skills and memory, and keeping things specific and direct helps simplify. There are many reasons to use the child's own words in your replies and summaries, not least because you are working with the concepts as they see them. Ultimately, there is a minimum level of maturity of thinking that children need for this kind of engagement, whatever accommodations the clinician is willing to make, and some psychologists have suggested that children under 7 years old may not be ready for such an approach (Piacentini & Bergman, 2001). Throughout childhood and adolescence, some processes underpinning social information processing are still developing, and thus maturity affects children's cognitive and social-emotional readiness to engage in reflection that drives behavioural change (Strait, McQuillin, Smith, & Englund, 2012).

Inclusive teamwork does not involve the same levels of intense and skilful questioning as are involved in psychological therapies. Children can learn to reflect on and talk about their interaction by doing it, as discussed above. Not all schools and families are happy to permit video recording, but if the appropriate facilities, consent and safeguarding is in place, video feedback can be a useful tool. Here children can watch clips of their own interaction and are encouraged to name the behaviours they see. A strengths-based approach is used, so that the children selectively watch positive moments where the group is demonstrating features of inclusive teamwork. The children watch and comment on what they see. Parsons, Cordier, Munro, and Joosten (2020) found that typically developing playmates benefited in terms of their pragmatic language skills from a group intervention with children with autism. They used video feedback to promote elements of pragmatic function in children's interaction and found that the children with typical development made significant gains.

What I have presented in this chapter is a framework for inclusive teamwork which is not based on models of normality and difference. It is not centred around bringing all children, including those with language disorder and pragmatic impairments, into similarity with other typically developing children. Instead, it is based on what all children need and appreciate when they collaborate: the collective skills and behaviours that facilitate teamwork.

References

Alexander, R. (2017). *Towards dialogic teaching: Rethinking classroom talk* (5th ed.). London: Dialogis UK.

Alison, E., & Alison, L. (2020). *Rapport: The four ways to read people*. Penguin.

Attwood, T. (2000). Strategies for improving the social integration of children with Asperger syndrome. *Autism: The International Journal of Research and Practice*, *4*(1), 85–100. https://doi.org/10.1177/1362361300004001006

Baines, E., Rubie-Davies, C., & Blatchford, P. (2009). Improving pupil group work interaction and dialogue in primary classrooms: Results from a year-long intervention study. *Cambridge Journal of Education*, *39*(1), 95–117. https://doi.org/10.1080/03057640802701960

Blank, M., Rose, S. A., & Berlin, L. J. (1978). *The language of learning: The preschool years*. New York: Grune & Stratton.

Blank, M., Rose, S. A., & Berlin, L. J. (2003). *Preschool Language Assessment Instrument (PLAI-2)* (2nd ed.). Austin, TX: ProEd.

Branigan, H. E., & Donaldson, D. I. (2019). Learning from learning logs: A case study of metacognition in the primary school classroom. *British Educational Research Journal*, *45*(4), 791–820. https://doi.org/10.1002/berj.3526

Coates, J. K., & Pimlott-Wilson, H. (2019). Learning while playing: Children's Forest School experiences in the UK. *British Educational Research Journal*, *45*(1), 21–40. https://doi.org/10.1002/berj.3491

Cordier, R., Munro, N., Wilkes-Gillan, S., Speyer, R., Parsons, L., & Joosten, A. (2019). Applying Item Response Theory (IRT) modeling to an observational measure of childhood pragmatics: The Pragmatics Observational Measure-2. *Frontiers in Psychology*, *10*(408). https://doi.org/10.3389/fpsyg.2019.00408

Dawes, L., Mercer, N., & Wegerif, R. (2000). *Thinking together: A programme of activities for developing thinking skills at KS2*. Birmingham: Imaginative Minds.

Denes, P. B., & Pinson, E. N. (1973). *The speech chain: The physics and biology of spoken language*. New York: Anchor Doubleday.

Flavell, J. H. (1979). Metacognition and cognitive monitoring: A new area of cognitive-developmental inquiry. *The American Psychologist*, *34*(10), 906–911. https://doi.org/10.1037/0003-066X.34.10.906

Gaile, J., & Adams, C. (2018). Metacognition in speech and language therapy for children with social (pragmatic) communication disorders: Implications for a theory of therapy. *International Journal of Language & Communication Disorders*, *53*(1), 55–69. https://doi.org/10.1111/1460-6984.12326

Gallagher, A. L., Murphy, C.-A., Conway, P. F., & Perry, A. (2019). Engaging multiple stakeholders to improve speech and language therapy services in schools: An appreciative inquiry-based study. *BMC Health Services Research, 19*(1), 226–217. https://doi.org/10.1186/s12913-019-4051-z

Garte, R. (2016). A sociocultural, activity-based account of preschooler intersubjectivity. *Culture & Psychology, 22*(2), 254–275. https://doi.org/10.1177/1354067x15621483

Gilbert, P. (Ed.). (2005). *Compassion: Conceptualisations, research and use in psychotherapy.* London: Routledge.

Harrist, A. W., & Waugh, R. M. (2002). Dyadic synchrony: Its structure and function in children's development. *Developmental Review, 22*(4), 555–592. https://doi.org/10.1016/S0273-2297(02)00500-2

Howe, C., Tolmie, A., Thurston, A., Topping, K., Christie, D., Livingston, K., . . . & Donaldson, C. (2007). Group work in elementary science: Towards organisational principles for supporting pupil learning. *Learning and Instruction, 17*(5), 549–563. https://doi.org/10.1016/j.learninstruc.2007.09.004

Johnson, D. W., & Johnson, R. T. (2005). New developments in social interdependence theory. *Genetic, Social, and General Psychology Monographs, 131*(4), 285–358. https://doi.org/10.3200/mono.131.4.285-358

Johnson, M., & Player, C. (2009). *Active listening for active learning: A mainstream resource to promote understanding, participation and personalised learning in the classroom.* Stafford: QEd.

Johnson, M., & Wintgens, A. (2017). *The selective mutism resource manual* (2nd ed.). London: Routledge.

Kamhi, A. G. (1987). Metalinguistic abilities in language-impaired children. *Topics in Language Disorders, 7*(2), 1–12.

Kennedy, H., Landor, M., & Todd, L. (Eds.). (2011). *Video interaction guidance: A relationship-based intervention to promote attunement, empathy and wellbeing.* London: Jessica Kingsley.

Kutnick, P., Blatchford, P., Baines, E., & Tolmie, A. (2014). *Effective group work in primary school classrooms: The SPRinG approach.* London: Springer.

Littleton, K., & Mercer, N. (2013). Educational dialogues. In K. Hall, T. Cremin, B. Comber, & L. C. Moll (Eds.), *International handbook of research on children's literacy, learning, and culture* (pp. 291–303). Oxford: Wiley.

Liu, Y., Carney, J. V., Kim, H., Hazler, R. J., & Guo, X. (2020). Victimization and students' psychological well-being: The mediating roles of hope and school connectedness. *Children and Youth Services Review, 108,* 104674. https://doi.org/10.1016/j.childyouth.2019.104674

Maione, L., & Mirenda, P. (2006). Effects of video modeling and video feedback on peer-directed social language skills of a child with autism. *Journal of Positive Behavior Interventions, 8*(2), 106–118.

Mercer, N. (1996). The quality of talk in children's collaborative activity in the classroom. *Learning and Instruction, 6*(4), 359–377. https://doi.org/10.1016/s0959-4752(96)00021-7

Mercer, N., Hennessy, S., & Warwick, P. (2019). Dialogue, thinking together and digital technology in the classroom: Some educational implications of a continuing line of inquiry. *International Journal of Educational Research, 97,* 187–199. https://doi.org/10.1016/j.ijer.2017.08.007

Merrick, R. (2009). *Children's views and speech and language therapy.* Bristol: University of the West of England.

Miller, W. R., & Rollnick, S. (2013). *Motivational interviewing: Helping people change* (3rd ed.). London: Guilford Press.

Parker, G. (2009). *Teamwork: 20 steps to success* (1st ed.). HRD Press.

Parsons, L., Cordier, R., Munro, N., & Joosten, A. (2020). Peer's pragmatic language outcomes following a peer-mediated intervention for children with autism: A randomised controlled trial. *Research in Developmental Disabilities, 99*, 103591. https://doi.org/10.1016/j.ridd.2020.103591

Piacentini, J., & Bergman, R. L. (2001). Developmental issues in cognitive therapy for childhood anxiety disorders. *Journal of Cognitive Psychotherapy, 15*(3), 165–182. https://doi.org/10.1891/0889-8391.15.3.165

Pomerantz, K. (2017). Finding attunement and promoting positive attachments. In A. Williams, T. Billington, D. Goodley, & T. Corcoran (Eds.), *Critical educational psychology* (pp. 200–208). Chichester: Wiley.

Robinson, S., Howlin, P., & Russell, A. (2017). Personality traits, autobiographical memory and knowledge of self and others: A comparative study in young people with autism spectrum disorder. *Autism, 21*(3), 357–367. https://doi.org/10.1177/1362361316645429

Rollnick, S., & Miller, W. R. (1995). What is motivational interviewing? *Behavioural and Cognitive Psychotherapy, 23*(4), 325–334. https://doi.org/10.1017/S135246580001643X

Semel, E., Wiig, E., & Secord, W. (2017). *Clinical evaluation of language fundamentals 5UK*. Bloomington, MN: Pearson.

Snape, L., & Atkinson, C. (2016). The evidence for student-focused motivational interviewing in educational settings: A review of the literature. *Advances in School Mental Health Promotion, 9*(2), 119–139. https://doi.org/10.1080/1754730X.2016.1157027

Snyder, C. R., Hoza, B., Pelham, W. E., Rapoff, M., Ware, L., Danovsky, M., . . . & Stahl, K. J. (1997). The development and validation of the Children's Hope Scale. *Journal of Pediatric Psychology, 22*(3), 399–421. https://doi.org/10.1093/jpepsy/22.3.399

Stallard, P. (2005). *A clinician's gudie to think good feel good: Using CBT with children and young people*. Chichester: Wiley.

Strait, G. G., McQuillin, S., Smith, B., & Englund, J. A. (2012). Using motivational interviewing with children and adolescents: A cognitive and neurodevelopmental perspective. *Advances in School Mental Health Promotion, 5*(4), 290–304. https://doi.org/10.1080/1754730X.2012.736789

Sun, J., & Vazire, S. (2019). Do people know what they're like in the moment? *Psychological Science, 30*(3), 405–414. https://doi.org/10.1177/0956797618818476

Thiemann, K. S., & Goldstein, H. (2001). Social stories, written text cues, and video feedback: Effects on social communication of children with autism. *Journal of Applied Behavior Analysis, 34*(4), 425–446. https://doi.org/10.1901/jaba.2001.34-425

Veenman, M. V. J., Van Hout-Wolters, B. H. A. M., & Afflerbach, P. (2006). Metacognition and learning: Conceptual and methodological considerations. *Metacognition and Learning, 1*(1), 3–14. https://doi.org/10.1007/s11409-006-6893-0

Wall, K. (2008). Understanding metacognition through the use of pupil views templates: Pupil views of learning to learn. *Thinking Skills and Creativity, 3*(1), 23–33. https://doi.org/10.1016/j.tsc.2008.03.004

Watson, D., Emery, C., Bayliss, P., Boushel, M., & McInnes, K. (2012). *Children's social and emotional wellbeing in schools: A critical perspective*. Bristol: Policy Press.

Webb, N. M. (2009). The teacher's role in promoting collaborative dialogue in the classroom. *British Journal of Educational Psychology, 79*(1), 1–28. https://doi.org/10.1348/000709908x380772

6 A framework for teaching inclusive teamwork

This chapter provides a framework for teaching inclusive teamwork. The structure for the programme is set out, describing the grouping of participants and role of the teacher and providing ideas for activities, which have aspects of effective communication as intrinsic to successful completion. Ideas for activities are organised according to their underlying rationale and objectives. A set of criteria is provided by which to measure a baseline and outcome, and this serves as a tool for discussion with the children during a course of sessions.

First, we should establish whether 'teaching' inclusive teamwork is necessary. Perhaps if we simply invite children to work in pairs or small groups, inclusive teamwork ensues? The answer to this is *not necessarily*. Readers may have encountered 'team-building' exercises in education and work contexts, where individuals are put together in teams to carry out cooperative games with the aim of engendering trust, promoting problem-solving and inspiring people to take a more collaborative approach to the tasks for which they are normally responsible. The games themselves may *or may not* be sufficient and effective in meeting these aims. I have seen free play used during lesson time to encourage interaction between children with SLCN and their peers. Again, attractive play materials may *or may not* be enough to facilitate positive interaction. Suitable tasks and materials are important, but the outcome depends upon the pre-existing dispositions and expectations of participants. Joint decision-making of groups who had participated in the SPRinG project was compared with control groups. Baines, Rubie-Davies, and Blatchford (2009) observed significantly higher levels of participation, engagement and discussion among groups that had received the focus on collaborative group working. Members of control groups were more often off-task, with individuals more often aggressive or ridiculing other members, disrupting and preventing group progress, in some cases splitting up rather than work together. Real success is the children not just interacting collaboratively but also knowing *how*, and the key to this success is coaching. The adult has a valuable role in guiding the participants in what to expect of themselves, observing closely and reflecting supportively with them.

Inclusive teamwork has the potential to offer meaningful support to children with communication disorders at a crucial time in their social development, and develop empathy and high-level thinking in their classmates. The definition of inclusive teamwork is that all members of a pair or small group are participating in

DOI: 10.4324/9781003201717-7

cooperative working. We are not necessarily looking for the participation of each group member to be the same in kind. Key behaviours simply need to be present *across the group as a whole*. These fall into three categories: *enjoying* – partners relate to each other and thus enjoy working together; *talking* – they talk to each other and understand each other; and *achieving* – they coordinate with each other effectively and feel pleased with their work.

The programme proposed here is based on the SPRinG approach (Baines, Blatchford, & Kutnick, 2017; Kutnick, Blatchford, Baines, & Tolmie, 2014). It has been adapted to actively include children with SLCN and practised in schools with children aged 7 to 14 years. An account of the way in which the programme has been structured, the observations that informed the development of the programme and the outcomes that have emerged as meaningful is presented later.

Timescales and participants

Children have seen benefits from inclusive teamwork after four sessions and have shown continued progress when pursuing the programme for a term or more. For comparison, the SPRinG programme ran for an academic year, whereas some targeted and specialist speech and language therapy programmes are limited to as few as four or six sessions. This chapter provides an outcome measure to evaluate the need for and impact of the sessions within a given timescale.

Where possible, the setting for inclusive teamwork sessions has been in a quiet space outside the classroom. Children were seated next to each other or at right angles with materials in front of them to facilitate good communication. Some of the sessions were conducted during the Covid 19 pandemic, which determined that children were forward-facing and avoiding contact with shared items. Some sessions were carried out via video conferencing, with the facilitator and each participant in a separate location.

It is important that participants can hear each other well. The acoustic environment will depend on many factors, including the design of the classroom (Shield, Greenland, & Dockrell, 2010), external environmental noise and class size as well as the activities of pupils. There is evidence that background talking has a negative impact on children's ability to carry out verbal tasks, and that children with SEN are differentially disadvantaged (Dockrell & Shield, 2006). Children with low confidence, a quiet voice, speech sound disorder, expressive language difficulties and/or comprehension difficulties will all benefit from an environment where participants' voices can be heard clearly. Reducing external stimuli also supports children's attention and concentration, which they need to engage and sustain during collaborative tasks.

Work has been in pairs, occasionally in threes, and facilitated by the author. In each pair, at least one (usually only one) of the children had identified SLCN. This chapter is written with reference to pairwork (using the term *partner*) but applies equally well to small group work. We know from the SPRinG project that working with a single partner tends to be easier than working in a group of three, and being part of a group of four is more challenging still. Sessions therefore initially involved a pair, and in some cases later sessions involved the addition of a third group participant. Often, one pairing was sustained across number of sessions, during which the children were able to get to know each other and develop a social bond. In other cases, two or three partners took turns to join the child with SCLN for the session. It gave the child with SLCN a range of personalities to interact with but took longer for the children to get to know each other.

How much choice should the children have in the composition of the pair or group? It is common for children to have a strong preference to work with a best friend or an aversion to working with a particularly disliked individual. Teachers tend to be in a position to have insights and make judgements about existing friendships, personalities and abilities, and will be inclined to draw on these when formulating groupings for small group work in class. Inclusive teamwork, however, is not (or at least should not be) dependent upon particular grouping. It is based on a principle regarding group cohesion – that to work together, children need a liking for each other, but that this liking need not be *personal* attraction. There is a *liking* component to group membership through participation. We saw in Chapter 3 how children can learn to get on through the experience of collaboration. Through understanding shared norms, perceiving shared goals and experiencing interdependence, children begin to psychologically identify with the group (Vaughan & Hogg, 2014). More crucial than selection and grouping of participants, then, is the teacher's role in devising, presenting and supervising tasks in such a way as to promote a spirit of cooperation and acceptance of each other.

Facilitating inclusive teamwork

There is a role for adult supervision throughout the session. I have referred to this supervisor as the teacher, but it could appropriately be a speech and language therapist, teacher or trained assistant. Inclusive teamwork emerges from children's opportunities to interact with each other *independently* from adults; at the same time, the children benefit from support and guidance in how to do this productively. The adult facilitating the programme therefore engages children in a cycle of reflection and adaptation, first briefing, then allowing children to practise with supervision but minimal intervention, then debriefing together. This cycle of briefing, activity and debriefing may be repeated a number of times. I run sessions of 30 minutes each comprising of two or three cycles. This keeps a practical focus, because the learning from one activity can be directly applied to the next.

In briefing the children at the beginning, it is the teacher's role to convey the goal of the task, so that all the children understand and share a sense of purpose. As we saw in Chapter 3, it is key to cooperation that they set out to achieve something 'together'. The clearer the presentation of the task, the less likely it is that the teacher will need to intervene during the activity. Briefing is an opportunity to highlight the criteria of inclusive teamwork inherent to the success of the task and draw these to the children's attention. However, for a first activity with a particular pair or group, I tend not to specify target behaviours, but rather observe carefully and then review using the measure of inclusive teamwork (provided later in this chapter) as a baseline measure. In subsequent briefing sessions, we then know which criteria to focus on and bring to children's attention. Children may at first lack the language or insight to talk about their teamwork. When they have put something into practice, however, there is something to praise, talk about and work on.

While the children complete the collaborative task, the teacher should observe carefully. I liken the role to a director of a film. The teacher is physically back from the scene but watching and listening to everything and ready to comment constructively at the end. Worley (2019) suggests that a facilitator is like a waiter – at hand with assistance if needed, but not intruding on the interaction. The teacher also looks after the time constraints on the session.

I find it essential to take notes, so that I can quote back to the children things they said or did, particularly when there are good examples of the criteria we are focusing on. This is a strengths-based approach to change and improvement. It works well if children recognise the extracts from their own interaction that are quoted back to them. Sometimes the children were so involved in the interaction that they were not aware of what they said or did. It is a useful facility, if possible, to video record the interaction and play back to the children selected clips which illustrate inclusive teamwork criteria in action. It takes time to edit video footage, but it is a powerful tool.

It is beneficial for children to experience the *need* for each of the criteria of inclusive teamwork. Then they will form their own view of what is important and what they are able to do. Sometimes they will only discover this by the adult refraining from intervening. For example, if at first there is a lack of initiative, it is worth waiting to see how the children solve the problem. If one child is dominating, it is worth watching to see the reaction of the other child. If conflict emerges, it is worth allowing the children the chance to try and resolve it themselves. All these experiences are useful to talk about afterwards. Like a referee, I have stepped in if a child is insulting to their partner, and also to cue a partner to take notice of something (e.g. 'What do you think of Sam's idea? Did you hear what he just said?'; 'Look at his face. What do you think he feels about that?'). For children that lack the vocabulary to talk about their interaction, some comments during the interaction can help them to understand what is happening (e.g. 'Good question'; 'You gave your reason, well done').

The debrief after the session is crucial to the programme. The aim is to encourage reflection. The children are usually able to reflect on whether they achieved the goal of the activity – 'Done it?' It is harder for them to talk about the quality of the cooperation. I find that many questions (such as, 'What went well?'; 'What could have been better?') will be answered with reference to the activity rather than the interaction. One way to introduce children to talking about teamwork is to give them examples from their own interaction and ask them to categorise. Table 6.1

shows examples of extracts on the left that children were asked to review, and on the right categories for the children to sort them into:

Table 6.1 Extracts and labels for children to match

—*I like to . . . say . . . play sports.* —*What did you say?*	encouraging
I think we need these screws to go in.	sharing ideas
Good job!	explaining
—*I want to go to Victoria Falls.* —*I'm going to the forest because it's safer there*	checking

After some examples, many children find it easier to find their own words to describe aspects of inclusive teamwork. There are often various words for similar concepts. *Explaining* means 'Give your reasons', 'Say why', 'Back up' what you say. *Keeping on task*, children call 'Helping', 'Concentrating', 'Focusing'. *Planning* children have called 'Getting organised', 'Being a leader', 'Strategizing'. It is valuable, wherever possible, to listen to the children's ways of expressing their ideas and experiences and work with these.

A measure of inclusive teamwork

An outcome measure of inclusive teamwork is useful to teachers and therapists for three reasons. First, we become more conscious of the things we measure. If inclusive teamwork is an important aspect of classroom life and children's experience of school, then teachers will want to draw attention to its importance and make sure it is not overlooked. Second, measuring aspects of teamwork reveals areas for potential improvement in order to tailor intervention. Third, they can be used to set and evaluate intervention and learning targets that are specific, measurable, achievable, realistic and time-bound. It helps if children themselves relate to the measure. They need to recognise the concepts and understand the way in which they are expressed. The more this is the case, the more able the children will be to reflect, engage their own motivation and effect meaningful changes.

The measure provided here contrasts with other outcome measures in the field of speech and language therapy, which have predominantly focused on the abilities or functional skills of the individual, such as Therapy Outcome Measures (TOM) (Enderby & John, 2019). Here we are not working with concepts such as impairment, independence or autonomy, and we are not comparing to a norm. We are looking at the collaboration between group members and the collective effect of their joint actions.

The criteria for inclusive teamwork are presented in Table 6.2, along with a description of groups where these features are missing. Each criterion can be rated

Table 6.2 Measure of inclusive teamwork

		Does at least one of you do this?	☑	*The alternative:*
Enjoy	1	*Pay attention* to your partner as well as the task. If your partner is not at first paying attention, get them involved. *Encourage* your partner to join in.	☐	You don't do it *together*. Your partner is *left out* or leaving themselves out.
	2	Show *initiative*. Share *ideas*.	☐	The work *doesn't get started*.
	3	*Respond. Respect* your partner's ideas and feelings.	☐	They feel *ignored* or *lack confidence*.
Talk	4	Put things into words: *tell* your partner, so they understand you.	☐	You are working *on your own*.
	5	Be prepared to *ask* questions and *explain*. Give reasons.	☐	You haven't taken everything into account. You may have *missed something* important.
	6	*Check* if you're not sure what someone said or what they meant.	☐	You *don't understand* or you *misunderstand* what your partner is saying.
Achieve	7	Know what you're trying to achieve. Judge when to stick with something and when to *move on*. Keep your partner *on task*.	☐	One or both of you go *off-task*.
	8	Work out a *plan* between you (like what you need to do first, and who's doing what).	☐	You *don't get very far*. You *go round in circles*.
	9	Reach a *conclusion* that you *both* contributed to.	☐	You *don't assert yourself* (you feel you have to agree) or you *quarrel*.
Total			/9	

as present or absent when observing or reflecting on a group activity, thus scoring between 0 and 9.

Inclusive teamwork activities

Putting inclusive teamwork into practice involves three interconnected dimensions, discussed in Chapter 5 and summarised in Table 6.2: enjoy, talk and achieve. They are cumulative inasmuch as achievement is supported by enjoyment and talking, but effective communication and team achievement also both feed in to enjoyment of the relationship, and focusing on what the group is setting out to achieve will strengthen mutual understanding. Thus, the order in the table does not designate importance or sequence in development. It helps if when they are carried out, the activities have one of the three dimensions as the primary focus, so that children are briefed and debriefed on one of these at a time.

Suggestions for activities are provided below. If possible, the teacher should tailor the content of the activities to participants' interests, age and maturity as well as the context and the demands of the curriculum. The better the teacher knows the skills and interests of the children, the better position they are in to do this. Children have pointed out that finding the interests they have in common with their partners helps them to bond and supports friendship. If tasks are well aligned to children's common interests, this is likely to capitalise on naturally occurring motivation to communicate. Moreover, we know that children are more likely to cooperate (rather than simply try to be self-reliant) on tasks that require resources and skills which are distributed across participants (Gross, Veistola, De Dreu, & Van Dijk, 2020). Many of the tasks given below involve distributing *resources* (providing partners with complementary materials), but if the teacher or pupils are also able to notice and highlight complementary *skills*, this is likely to promote inclusive teamwork and enhance the programme. The activities provided below are set out according to underlying ideas with a range of examples which can be adapted and creatively exploited.

Teamwork is about working towards a shared goal: children perceive the shared goal and monitor their interactions in relation to it. Activities which best lend themselves to inclusive teamwork working have certain qualities. They tend to be intrinsically rewarding (not reliant on extrinsic rewards), to have an element of exploration and/or open-ended problem-solving (with no single right answer) and do not encourage competition between the participants (Damon & Phelps, 1989). Open-ended tasks are ideal for mixed-attainment group work if they have a 'low floor, high ceiling', that is, everyone in the group can begin the activity and work at their own level with the potential to challenge themselves (Francis, Taylor, & Tereshchenko, 2020). They also foster respect and responsibility in peer relations (Boaler, 2008).

Enjoy

Children collaborate when there is an intrinsic reward for doing so, and this is often simply finding it fun. When children enjoy each other's company, they pay attention to each other as well as the task. They are relating to each other and experiencing connectedness. They don't necessarily have to start off as 'friends'; they build a positive relationship through the enjoyment of initiating and responding, verbally or non-verbally. One child may be slower to engage attention or less sure how to start the task, in which case it helps if their partner shows initiative and encourages their partner to join in. Partners share ideas, are responsive to each other and respect each other's ideas and feelings.

If this is our aim, it helps to begin with activities that require very little verbal explanation. Then the emphasis can stay on the interaction rather than issues around comprehension. The lower the language demand, the easier it is for children with communication difficulties to participate. An activity that gets children initiating and responding provides the conditions for building trust and enjoyment. The key to coaching them is helping them to recognise when they are doing positive things – facing the right way, being observant, showing that they are listening, responding and thinking about the other person.

1   Sharing experiences

Joint attention is a prerequisite for communication. By joint attention, I mean two people paying attention to the same stimulus, this providing a reference point for their interaction with each other.

> Sensory experiences can provide a powerful shared stimulus and naturally trigger interaction. So, for example, I have provided children with sealed openable containers with smells inside and asked them, 'What can you smell? Do you like it? What does your partner think of it?' I use empty jars that contain a lingering smell of such things as lemon zest, garlic, ginger, crisps, aftershave, antiseptic, engine oil.

The children tend to demonstrably share their feelings about whether they like or dislike the smell, and try to identify what it is. Some children talk about the associations that the smells have for them, like 'My nan's house', 'My mum's cooking'. Because reactions are personal, we can encourage children's empathy and respect in the face of differences. A 'right' answer exists in terms of what has been in the jar, but it is open-ended too, as children have the freedom to comment on what it 'smells like' to them. Even without the language, this is an interactive activity, as partners can watch and compare each other's non-verbal reactions.

> Sound can also be a shared stimulus to promote interaction. I have used randomised recorded sounds, such as a Sound Lotto game, for the children to listen and identify, 'What's that?' This can be done as a non-verbal activity if there is a board with corresponding pictures to match. Example sounds are particular instruments, animals, tools and gadgets in use.

Children tend to acknowledge what their partners are thinking with non-verbal cues and often talk as well.

It is worth noting that some children with SLCN have co-occurring sensory processing issues. Smells and sounds can be overwhelming or preoccupying. I have worked with children who, once they have found a smell they like, have not wanted to put the jar down, and also with children who wanted to avoid sampling sensations, especially if they might be intense. It is therefore important that children can regulate their own activity and respect each other's wishes.

Children with social communication difficulties are sometimes slow to transition in to activities and may not be comfortable enough to pay attention using conventional eye gaze. Children find their own approach with each other and learn to interpret the signals that indicate their partner is, or is not, listening and interested.

2   Brainstorming

Having the confidence to be creative and show initiative is key to many other aspects of collaboration. If children are slow to initiate, this may be because they are fearful of negative evaluation, or words and ideas might need a trigger. In either case, it is a useful exercise to ask children to brainstorm, that is, between them to generate as many words or ideas as possible without censorship or evaluation. Brainstorming is an activity which can result in more creativity the more heterogeneous the group, which can be an advantage if children initially have little in common.

One activity for brainstorming uses a ball. We call it *word tennis*, if children are familiar with tennis as a game. The children pass a tennis ball back and forth between each other, for example, rolling it to each other across the desk. As they roll, they say a word. Their partner listens, and on their roll, they give the word that it makes them think of. Thus, they are free to associate and there are no right answers, no category constraints; everyone makes their own connections. For example, if the starter word is *fish*, the partner may say *chips* or *sea* or *salmon* . . . On each turn, the child gives a word related to the last one and passes the tennis ball to their partner. The starter word can be anything. Random examples of starter words I have used are: *ice, helmet, China, train, pancake, cinema, Egyptian, cupcake.* You can elaborate the game by inviting children to explain the connection (e.g. I thought of *salmon* because that's my favourite *fish*).

Another activity is to give children a category (or invite them to choose a category) to name items from. Provide a squeaker to sound if there is repetition, and then the round stops. The children have to listen carefully to each other to avoid repetition. This is a useful exercise for vocabulary and word finding, because it supports memory and recall to make semantic connections, and examples trigger more ideas. Examples of categories that I use with children aged 7 to 11 include *foods, clothes, shapes, pets, games, things in a pencil case, boys' names.* Examples of categories that I have used with young people aged 11–14 include: *unhealthy foods, pancake toppings, makes of car, brands of make-up, clothes shops, tools, jobs.*

A physical object can be a useful focus of attention, and one activity is to pass an object round, thinking laterally about the possible uses for it. This could be a common object that has come to the end of its life, like a sock, a light bulb or a cotton reel. In this case the children are encouraged to imagine how it could be reused. Alternatively, it could be an unusual item that the children are unlikely to recognise. I have used specialist pieces of camping equipment, rare kitchen gadgets and antique and historical items, such as a snuff box and a toasting fork. In this case, the children are encouraged to observe and explore the item carefully, being both imaginative and deductive in their thinking. It is helpful to celebrate all the children's ideas and the thinking that goes into them; and it may not even be necessary to reveal the 'right answer', since this is not the goal of the exercise.

On these brainstorming activities, some children may be more forthcoming than others, and some may rely on others to take the initiative, so that they can follow from an example. As was stated in Chapter 5, it would be simplistic to consider *equal* participation to be the marker of good teamwork. However, it could be that children need some recognition and encouragement for their participation. Jolliffe (2007) suggested giving tokens to group members. When they talk, they put a token in the middle of the table. They can speak as long as their tokens last. I have found that the advantage of this technique is that it gives over responsibility to the children to time their turns. It means that they can delay their turn if they want to and wait for ideas from others, and it provides visual feedback to children about their participation.

When children are playing these games, they are learning how to give responses which are contingent on those of their partner. Listening and responding are built in to the success of the task. Some children with SLCN easily go off-topic. Conversation can be tangential, due to comprehension difficulties or social communication difficulties. For these children, it is a helpful aspect of the activities that the topic is made explicit.

Some children with communication difficulties perseverate, that is, they get stuck in a particular train of thought, or a previously used word interferes with subsequent word finding. Brainstorming can reveal these problems but also help children with them. One boy could think of no other *fizzy drinks* after naming Fanta, until examples from his partner helped him to move on. Word finding and vocabulary can greatly depend upon experience and interest, and it can be fascinating for children to discover each other's strengths. One 14-year-old boy could think of almost no types of *weather* or *countries* but got on a never-ending roll with his partner with makes of *car* and also with *tools*, as carpentry was a much-loved hobby.

3   Copying

If we are aiming for children to take notice of each other and enjoy each other's company, then it helps to draw their attention to non-verbal aspects of communication. Tasks which require copying each other involve being aware of each other, watching, listening, tracking the object of the other person's attention and using imagination to anticipate what they might do next. These are all qualities which support language acquisition, and can also be fun to do. Watching others is often a first step towards joining in for children who want to play together (Robinson, Anderson, Porter, Hart, & Wouden-Miller, 2003), and it is likely to have an important function in mature social interaction.

> One imitation task that I have frequently used is to give children matching boxes of identical contents to explore, and invite them to 'Do the same' as each other. Percussion instruments work well, for example, a handbell, castanets, a maraca, a ratchet.

The children coordinate what they do, mutually deciding how long to spend on each item and when to move on to what. They also look to each other for ideas on what to do with the items, especially when one item makes different sounds in different ways.

> Children have enjoyed drawing together. One child is invited to draw a simple figure on paper or a whiteboard, with the instruction for their partner to 'Draw the same'. Younger children have drawn, for example, *a sun, an apple, a robot, a cartoon bomb.*

Although this is potentially a non-verbal task, children tend to talk, and this is to be encouraged. Older children are asked to draw a diagram with their partner that they recall from lessons, explaining what it shows.

> An activity suggested by Baines et al. (2017, p. 102) for developing sensitivity and awareness of others is *Mirror Mirror*, where one child acts out everyday activities, and their partner follows the actions as their mirror image. As a warm-up and to give children ideas, we have talked about mirrors and practised miming the steps involved in, for example, getting up and getting ready for school (waking up, stretching or yawning, brushing teeth, serving breakfast, styling hair, waving goodbye).
>
> I have also given matching sets of construction items to partners, such as a small selection of Lego® bricks or any other clip-together pieces. One builds while the other follows and copies the process to achieve a matching result.

Again, this is essentially non-verbal, just requiring watching and showing, but children are likely to put into words what they are thinking and wanting to check.

Some children with communication difficulty, not least those with speech sound disorder, are greatly troubled by issues around intelligibility. The non-verbal element of these imitation exercises can give these children respite from this area of struggle and focus them on other enjoyable aspects of interaction. For some, drawing, building and manipulating objects may present their own challenges, but for others they could be in their element, feeling confident and having fun.

4   Answering questions

Another step in highlighting the enjoyment of interaction for children is helping them to listen to each other. Finding things in common supports friendship, and so does the ability to recognise and respect difference. Providing them with questions to ask each other has been a way of helping children enjoy getting to know each other. The most convenient way of providing questions is in written form, if at least one member of the group is able to read well enough for this. The advantage of written questions is that children can work through them independently at their own pace. If reading is a barrier to participation, however, the questions can be spoken to them or made available on audio. Each child responds to the question and they compare their answers. Children are briefed to expect similarities and differences. Children learn to recognise and respect these in a way that supports the development of empathy and values diversity.

Questions can be designed to help children get to know each other by presenting themes that they care about, such as questions about their preferences: 'What is your favourite [colour/food/sport]?'; experiences: 'Have you ever [been on a bus/eaten sushi/fallen asleep in class]?' or imagination, such as 'What is your dream holiday?'; 'Which celebrity would you most like to meet?'

Children can also discuss their answers to quiz questions or compose quiz questions for each other. The success of the latter relies on predicting what their partner may know and be interested in. The aim is to find questions that children do know the answers to, in order to draw attention to their strengths, especially where these are complementary.

Some children are more comfortable with factual questions than with conversation, and for others it is the other way around. The teacher should aim to find the children's comfort zone and start there. Yes/No questions, as long as they are comprehended, are easier to answer than open-ended ones. I tend to use these at the start and encourage elaboration. For example, if a child answers 'Yes' to 'Have you ever been bitten by an animal?', the listener is likely to be interested to hear or ask more about this story. When questions are personal, there should be an element of choice about how and whether to answer. 'I'm not sure' is a viable answer if children wish. The teacher should brief the children to ensure that they (a) invite each other but do not put *pressure* on each other to talk and (b) respond in a trustworthy and supportive way to anything that their partner says. In my experience, children have found questions to be light-hearted, and enjoy discovering each other's answers, both the commonalities and the differences.

Talk

This dimension is about the quality of verbal communication between the children. One component of this is putting ideas into words, and another is being willing to question ideas. Being willing to question has two benefits. It encourages children to explain and reason, leading to a higher quality of thought and discussion. It also enables them to check back with each other and clear up misunderstandings.

5   Debating

In the last section, we saw how questions get children expressing their views, sharing their experiences and their knowledge in a way that encourages them to relate to each other.

Questions can also be effective in stimulating debate when children are invited to give their opinions. Examples of questions that I have used to get a debate going include, *Are zoos cruel? Are sharks dangerous? Is life better now than it was in 1945? Is there such a thing as too much screen time? Are haircuts important?* Children have tended to give a simple Yes/No response at first. However, if they are briefed to express their reasons for their views, they elaborate. This helps all parties to see other sides of the argument and progress their ideas.

Many children with SLCN have difficulty with verbal reasoning. It is common for children to need support learning to link ideas and use language such as '*Why?*' '*Because . . .*' '*If*'. There are other terms for reasoning such as '*Until*', '*Unless*' and '*Otherwise*' that can be even harder still to comprehend and express. The way in is to work with topics that relate closely to children's interests and experience. They will be more confident and their ideas will be better formulated. There are always simpler versus more complicated ways of phrasing ideas, and it helps if partners check in with each other and learn to adapt what they say to suit their listener.

When debating, I have found it useful to reflect with the children on the distinction between *fact* and *opinion*. We can experience our own strong views as fact when they are only opinions, and facts that we are uncertain of can feel like loosely held views. Realising the nature of opinion is an essential step in dealing with conflict and also in being receptive to the arguments of others. Children benefit from being provided with information in preparation for a debate, particularly children with expressive difficulties and limited vocabulary. In this respect, it helps if inclusive teamwork is integrated into the themes and topics of ongoing classwork.

Children whose speech is unclear often have the experience of being ignored. People listen but if they don't understand, it seems to them more comfortable at the time to give a generic acknowledgement or feign understanding rather than keep asking for clarification. However, it is kinder, better for speech and language development and a feature of more effective communication to find a way of somehow reaching intelligibility. It is hugely helpful and something to encourage when children check with each other as to what they said.

6   Directing

In inclusive teamwork, mutual understanding is a task shared between the speaker and the listener. Partners involve each other and work together. There are a number of types of task requiring the children to direct each other. These involve communication and sensitivity to the other's needs. The tasks bring home the fact that other people don't necessarily know what you know; they reveal the importance of explaining, and also, as a listener, the value of checking back to make sure you have understood correctly.

There are many party games based around blindfolds, because it is a fun way to experiment with reliance on a partner. Partners take turns to shut their eyes or accept a blindfold while the other guides them

(a)   around an obstacle course (one that has been risk-assessed for the purpose) or
(b)   to retrieve certain items, for example, percussion instruments from a table top, or bean bags and hoops in a gym hall.

There is constant feedback for the child speaking; they can see whether the messages they are wishing to convey are being correctly understood, and they learn to alter what they say accordingly.

In *barrier games* each child has matching sets of equipment – pictures or objects, toys or instruments, and a barrier (something which can stand up on the table, such as an open book, a briefcase) hides their work from their partner's. Behind the barrier (in earshot but their actions out of view), one child carries out an activity, putting into words what they are doing. The partner must listen and replicate using their own set of materials. At the end, the barrier is removed to bring both into view and compare. This provides visual feedback on the accuracy of their communication. Examples are

(a) Matching sounds: each child has a matching array of sound-making objects, such as percussive instruments, a bicycle bell, a pencil sharpener. One child makes a sound with one, and the partner holds up the matching item.

(b) Tableau: each child has a matching set of toys. One example I use is a Playmobil® pirate and seagull, rope, bottle, boat and bucket. The child sets the items up as a scene, and describes this to their partner to replicate (e.g. 'Put the pirate in the boat', 'He has a rope in his hand').

(c) Drawing: one child draws, while giving a running commentary for the other to follow.

In a method similar to barrier games, children can also give instructions either from an illustrated instruction card or, alternatively, using a completed item made earlier as an example. Their partner meanwhile has access to the requisite materials. The child describes in such a way that the other can assemble/arrange the materials to match the instructions. As long as the child with the instructions does not show them until the task is achieved, the process remains focused on the team's verbal communication. Examples are

(a) Lego® instructions for a simple design;

(b) a photo of an arrangement of objects or toys;

(c) a diagram showing *Qwirkle*™ tablets (a game by MindWare®) or other coloured shapes in a particular pattern;

d) a clip-together action figure to replicate;

e) a screw-together vehicle; and

f) a paper plane.

If children have problems with accurate use of language, then these activities will highlight these. This is helpful to the extent that it promotes clarification and self-correction. It is not unusual for children with language disorder to muddle up *in front/behind*, for example, or miss out key information while focusing on selected details. I have found that even the most self-conscious children have been willing and determined to correct their own errors, finding these games a safe and motivating environment in which to do so. Many children have word finding and vocabulary difficulties, which mean they don't say quite what they intended. Good listeners will reiterate what they heard, correcting the error or checking what their partner means.

It is important to be aware, however, that communication difficulty can cause anxiety. Comprehension difficulties are more detrimental to participation than expressive difficulties. If children are unable to understand what is said, they rely on the non-verbal context for a way in to the interaction. Some children also have specific anxiety about talking. If children are anxious, they need to feel secure. For some children, this might mean doing without the blindfold or barrier and utilising the non-verbal context to support mutual understanding and interaction, as children can demonstrate what they mean.

7   Guessing

Guessing games focus on children's ability to describe. In these activities, one child has access to some information that their partner does not; they give clues or answer questions until their partner has worked it out. It's quite an artificial exercise, not to be used with everyone: some children don't have the maturity to hold back the information to be guessed (or don't see the point) and give it away straight away. However, it is useful because it involves descriptive skills, questioning skills and also logic. The idea of helping is intrinsic to the exercise, and in order to keep team members on track, the child needs to monitor progress and give encouraging feedback.

One guessing game that I have used is *emotion charades*. Given a picture from a story book, one partner enacts the emotion (e.g. a little pig when the big bad wolf has fallen in the cooking pot; a baby owl waiting for his mother; a boy being evacuated from a war zone) for the other to identify the emotion (pleased, scared). When they are correct, the child reveals the picture, showing the illustrated emotion and the context.

Children can also identify words from each other's verbal definitions: one child has a random word or picture on a card, or an object in a box, to define (such as *lobster, wolf, jellyfish, penguin, statue, pirate, farmer, spy*) for their partner to guess. If the child is asked to draw rather than define the word, then the partner guessing must do more of the talking and ask questions.

The classic game of *Guess Who*™ (from Hasbro® Gaming) falls into this category too. In this game, the child progressively narrows down options from a range of possible faces by asking their partner Yes/No questions, for example 'Is it a man?', 'Are they wearing glasses?'

Children can be presented with a problem to solve by deduction. One of my favourite activities is to present them with a hygienically prepared waste paper basket or recycle bin belonging to a fictitious person. The children are asked to rummage in the bin, explore the contents and work out what we know about the person and what they have been doing. Items in the bin can include transport tickets or receipts, event programmes, recognisable packaging for food or other items. This is a good context for exploring the difference between deduction and inference. There will be some things that we know for sure, and other things that we can work out using our imagination. The language involved in expressing these ideas (such as *must, might, could*) can be complex and subtle; the presence of props can guide the conversation and support comprehension.

Children with comprehension difficulties are guessing a lot of the time, and so are the partners of children with speech and expressive language difficulties. Older children tell me, 'I'm guessing' when they are not sure if their responses are correct, and it is hard for them to be confident. The activities mentioned earlier are helpful to the extent that they encourage children to persist and use logical deduction to arrive at answers. For some children with social communication difficulties, it also highlights the reality that not everyone knows what you know and the importance of explaining to others what is obvious to you.

8   Pooling information

Information gap exercises are widely used in teaching languages, and the technique is valuable for encouraging interaction and collaboration. Each child is given a piece of partial information which they put together with the information given to their partner to solve a problem. Collaborative work often involves children taking complementary roles and pooling resources. These activities draw children's attention to their interdependence and encourages effective information exchange.

Children can be encouraged to work together using paired resources. Examples of these that I have used successfully are pictures of fictional couples (e.g. Sherlock Holmes and Dr Watson, Hiccup and Toothless), celebrities (e.g. Prince Harry and Meghan Markle), wildlife, such as male and female birds/animals or predator and prey. The children put what they have together with what their partner has to make a match. If using pictures alone, this is a non-verbal task and a context in which spontaneous exchange of comments and questions is likely and natural.

Pairs of pictures can be used for Spot the Difference. This is a verbal exercise if the children keep their slightly differing pictures hidden from each other and aim to describe in detail in order to find the differences. Partners can compare the pictures directly at the end for feedback on their accuracy.

Along the lines of the drawing activity listed under *Directing*, children can be given complementary halves of a picture to complete. For this, I have used a map of the country for children to add weather symbols using information about the forecast.

Speech and language difficulties often mean that information conveyed is initially vague or incomplete. In these activities, completeness of the information is the goal of the task, so children have the incentive to question and check with each other. It draws attention to children's interdependence, and the need to take notice of each other's contributions. They acquire strategies for clearing up ambiguity as well as the confidence to do so.

Achieve

One can have fun and communicate effectively but still not get anywhere with a task. Children can find themselves going round in circles, stuck or losing interest. The third step in inclusive teamwork is to achieve the mutual goal. This involves several components. It is not uncommon for children to lose their focus, either because they forget the goal or become distracted or preoccupied by something else. In inclusive teamwork, children have a role in keeping each other on task, understanding the shared aim and noticing each other's efforts (or lack of them). Together, children judge when to stick with something and when to move on. Children make a plan between them, for example about what to do first, or who is doing what. Finally, they need to recognise when the task is complete. It is a sign of good inclusive teamwork if children reach a conclusion that both partners contributed to.

Children can be briefed to try and 'agree'. However, without attention to the processes involved in discussing and understanding each other, this can lead to acquiescence and lack of assertiveness, with one partner simply going along with what the other says. As we saw in Chapter 3, children do not need to resolve differences on the spot. Teamwork can leave them thinking about things beyond the end of the session. The important thing is their understanding of the shared goal and their willingness to work mutually towards this.

9   Ranking

Ranking involves making comparisons and requires children to arrive at a judgement. Children can be asked to choose the 'best' from an array of options or asked to put items in order. If it is done well, it will involve giving opinions and elaborating on reasons.

One example of a ranking activity is for children to decide on a meal they would both like. Children select from *Tummy Ache*™ puzzle pieces (a game by Orchard Toys®) and assemble a meal that they would both be happy to eat. Pictures of food from magazines would also work.

This process stimulates children to express views, such as what they like to eat and also sometimes to share knowledge, such as what is healthy or how to manage allergies.

Another ranking activity involving choices and judgements is to ask the children 'What is a good present?' for someone they both know.

The children make suggestions and share their knowledge about the other person, their interests and perhaps what they have already. Providing items to choose from can cut out the need for children to generate ideas, but I have found that they sometimes then arrive at a decision quickly without reasoning or discussing.

I have involved children in discussing their personal reactions to stimuli, such as 'Which is the funniest joke?' 'Which book would you most want to read?' 'Which film would you most want to watch?'

Setting out physical examples in front of them focuses the activity. Discussing media involves making predictions about the genre and the story and also asking questions about what your partner has tried before and might prefer.

Another activity is to invite children to organise items on a factual basis. For example, I have given children model animals that can be arranged into a number of food chains (e.g. *fish, seal, polar bear; grass, antelope, lion*). They have also been given the planets of the solar system to order.

These tasks are not open ended if there is a 'right answer' but can work well if children have reciprocal knowledge.

Picture cards are useful for ranking, such as selections from *Top Trumps*® packs. For example, from a limited array of Top Trumps *Wonders of the World* cards, children have been asked (somewhat fantastically) 'Where would you recommend for a school trip?' From *Battleships*, children were asked to rate 'Which was the best battleship (and why)?' From Predators, children were asked, 'Which is the most dangerous animal?'

I have found that children with little experience of working together often take an easy way out on these tasks. They know that they can avoid disagreement by deferring to their partner or by settling on a conclusion without giving reasons. The real benefit of the task is to be had in engaging in discussion and reasoning, giving consideration to all the alternatives and still managing to reach a consensus. This is something that children can be guided towards.

10 Solving problems

There are a number of steps that we go through to solve a complex problem – after understanding the problem and analysing it, we suggest solutions, evaluate the possible outcomes and settle on what we believe to be the best plan of action (Jolliffe, 2007). When we present problem scenarios to children, some of the analysis has been done for them; the challenge for them is to focus on the options available – generating ideas, reasoning, predicting and choosing between them.

> Baines et al. (2017, p. 111) suggest a number of predicaments for children to consider and discuss what they would do, such as '*Your house is on fire. You have time to save two things*', '*Someone keeps picking on your best friend*'. In Talking About Secondary School™ (Black Sheep Press®, 2004), problem scenarios are illustrated. Children are invited to consider and evaluate a student's options when, for example, they are not sure which books to bring to school or they are stuck on a piece of work in class.

I have found children to be the most confident in problem situations which are close to their experience. There is a good deal of verbal reasoning around stating the options and justifying a plan of action.

Children lack confidence if they don't have a track record of problem-solving and success. Some children with SLCN in particular have got used to receiving help or being told what to do, without necessarily working things out for themselves. Some of my work with children has focused on the element of initiative – the willingness to generate ideas and persevere. They have also needed to work on testing out ideas, taking notice of what they find and reviewing progress accordingly. This is a basic skill not only in science but also in collaborative working at the same time.

11 Constructing

Children can be given the task of making something and the requisite equipment provided. If there is no set of instructions or real example of the finished item, then children are required to organise themselves and make choices about how to approach the task. Distributing different items of equipment to different children can encourage collaboration as they need to pool their resources.

I have given children components from a clip-together electrical set with the instruction to 'Make something happen' or 'Make the bulb light up'. I have given children the components of a vehicle that can be powered by a rubber band, with the instruction to 'Make it go'. I have given children a set of Jenga bricks, with the instruction 'Make a tower as high as you can' or 'Build a pyramid'. I have given children Geomag™ with the instruction to 'Make a building that can survive an earthquake'.

Another way of engaging children in joint construction is to distribute pieces of a simple but age-appropriate jigsaw puzzle between them. This is essentially a non-verbal task, but there is strategy involved in working together, which the teacher can brief children on beforehand and review afterwards.

Some children with SLCN love a practical task; they see a way of getting round their verbal difficulties and they are in their element. However, it is not uncommon for difficulties with fine motor coordination to accompany speech and language difficulties. Children learn to bear their own skill set in mind when approaching work with a partner. The better they know each other, the more appropriately they can suggest and volunteer for roles.

12 Thinking philosophically

Questions which are philosophical by nature can stimulate children to collaborate as they initiate and compare their ideas. Children can be encouraged to think creatively and to respect and respond to each other's contributions, however diverse.

Worley (2019) has provided teaching materials and strategies to encourage philosophical thinking in children. For example, he provides a story about ants who are asking about the meaning of life (p. 69–72). He also suggests enacting a scenario in which a child tries to lose something, in order to ask 'What is it to lose something?' (p. 88). After the initial stimulus, the children are allocated time to discuss their answers among themselves.

Worley gives good examples of how closed questions can be used at first to engage participation (e.g. 'Are ants just food for anteaters?'), and then follow-up questions can open up thinking around children's original answer. This helps children with comprehension as well as participation.

Philosophy involves defining words and exploring more than one meaning, which can help children with weak vocabulary. Children's understanding of vocabulary is sometimes limited not only in range but also in depth, so there are words that they understand in a limited sense. For example, one teenager had understood *rare* as 'valuable', and *source* as a 'source of information', but not of heat or of a river. Discussion with examples is key to elaborating understanding of words across different contexts.

Worley's strategy of presenting a *task question* ('What are ants *for*?') helps 'anchor' the children. By this, he means having a single question for the group to answer, as it draws children's ideas together, helps them to make connections and think more deeply. This is supportive in particular of children whose attention wanders and those with comprehension difficulties.

Final reflections

Rarely does one size fit all. Teachers adapt their lessons, and speech and language therapists must tailor their interventions to fit with children's priorities and interests. The framework of the inclusive teamwork programme is designed with this flexibility in mind. Inclusive teamwork is fun because it involves creativity and responsiveness. It is effective because children learn to communicate in ways that are important to them. It has impact because children gain positive academic and social identities.

The material in this book lends itself to taking a person-centred approach, and at the same time focuses teachers on the features of peer interaction that are absolutely crucial for all children's inclusion, school achievement and self-esteem. Peer interaction plays a significant part in children's lives, and between the ages of 7 and 14, participation becomes increasingly important to them. Given the right opportunities, children learn to engage, communicate and work well together with others. This book has set out the theoretical and practical reasons for supporting children in this learning process. Since communication is a collective endeavour, communication difficulty is something that all partners must productively work together to alleviate. When children have SLCN, interventions focusing on their impairments and deficits do not necessarily fit with their priorities and perspectives. It is the case for all children that relationships form an important basis for learning and achievement. For children with SLCN in particular, social connectedness has the potential to mitigate the risk of poor psychosocial outcomes. Children can and do develop the awareness to reflect upon their own inclusive teamwork and are motivated to improve levels of collaboration. This chapter has outlined the framework and content of a programme to enable children and young people to do this.

The three dimensions of inclusive teamwork – enjoyment, talking and achievement – apply to the interaction between facilitator and participants too. Rapport and enjoyment, careful listening and good communication between teacher and children all contribute to the briefing and debriefing sections of the programme. A good teacher will identify which features of the interaction to pick up on, open up a course of action in which all the children play an active part, and guide them towards their own goals. Children and young people will continue to teach us what is important, help us to reflect on what works and identify the markers of the kind of inclusion and teamwork that is meaningful to them.

References

Baines, E., Blatchford, P., & Kutnick, P. (2017). *Promoting effective group work in the primary classroom: A handbook for teachers and practitioners* (2nd ed.). Abingdon: Routledge.

Baines, E., Rubie-Davies, C., & Blatchford, P. (2009). Improving pupil group work interaction and dialogue in primary classrooms: Results from a year-long intervention study. *Cambridge Journal of Education, 39*(1), 95–117. https://doi.org/10.1080/03057640802701960

Boaler, J. (2008). Promoting "relational equity" and high mathematics achievement through an innovative mixed-ability approach. *British Educational Research Journal, 34*(2), 167–194. https://doi.org/10.1080/01411920701532145

Damon, W., & Phelps, E. (1989). Critical distinctions among three approaches to peer education. *International Journal of Educational Research, 13*(1), 9–19. https://doi.org/10.1016/0883-0355(89)90013-X

Dockrell, J., & Shield, B. M. (2006). Acoustical barriers in classrooms: The impact of noise on performance in the classroom. *British Educational Research Journal, 32*(3), 509–525. Retrieved from www.jstor.org/stable/30032680

Enderby, P., & John, A. (2019). *Therapy outcome measure user guide*. Guildford: J&R Press.

Francis, B., Taylor, B., & Tereshchenko, A. (2020). *Reassessing 'ability' grouping: Improving practice for equity and attainment*. Abingdon, Oxon: Routledge.

Gross, J., Veistola, S., De Dreu, C. K. W., & Van Dijk, E. (2020). Self-reliance crowds out group cooperation and increases wealth inequality. *Nature Communications, 11*(1), 5161. https://doi.org/10.1038/s41467-020-18896-6

Jolliffe, W. (2007). *Cooperative Learning in the classroom: Putting it into practice*. London: Paul Chapman.

Kutnick, P., Blatchford, P., Baines, E., & Tolmie, A. (2014). *Effective group work in primary school classrooms: The SPRinG approach*. London: Springer.

Robinson, C. C., Anderson, G. T., Porter, C. L., Hart, C. H., & Wouden-Miller, M. (2003). Sequential transition patterns of preschoolers' social interactions during child-initiated play: Is parallel-aware play a bidirectional bridge to other play states? *Early Childhood Research Quarterly, 18*(1), 3–21. https://doi.org/10.1016/s0885-2006(03)00003-6

Shield, B., Greenland, E., & Dockrell, J. (2010). Noise in open plan classrooms in primary schools: A review. *Noise & Health, 12*(49), 225–234. https://doi.org/10.4103/1463-1741.70501

Vaughan, G., & Hogg, M. (2014). *Social psychology* (7th ed.). London: Pearson Education.

Worley, P. (2019). *The if machine: 30 lesson plans for teaching philosophy* (2nd ed.). London: Bloomsbury Education.

Index

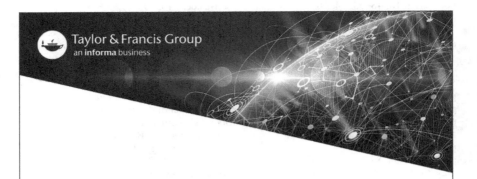